Requiem

CW00539816

The Killing of Robert Nairac

Requiem for a Spy

The Killing of Robert Nairac

Anthony Bradley

MERCIER PRESS

MERCIER PRESS
PO Box 5, 5 French Church Street, Cork
24 Lower Abbey Street, Dublin 1

First published in March 1993

ISBN 1 85635 020 7

A CIP is available for this book from the British Library.

For Rita
Who confers a thousand blessings

Printed in Ireland by Colour Books Ltd.

Introduction

Armed soldiers posted guard on Dublin's Special Criminal Court on the grey October day in 1977 when Liam Townson, a 24-year-old joiner and alleged IRA killer went on trial for the murder of a British officer, Captain Robert Nairac. Townson, from Meigh, County Armagh pleaded not guilty. He also denied possessing a firearm with intent to endanger life.

The court heard that 29-year-old Nairac, an undercover SAS officer, had been seized from the car park of the Three Steps Inn, Drumintee, South Armagh and taken to a field where he was beaten and kicked by his captors before being shot dead by Townson. Townson, an IRA man on the run, had been brought from Dundalk at around midnight on Saturday, 14 May 1977, to carry out the killing.

He was found guilty of both offences and sentenced to penal servitude for life on the murder charge. He was also given a five year jail sentence, to run concurrently, on the firearms charge. The sentences came at the end of a controversial trial in which the defence made widespread claims of threatening and abusive behaviour by detectives involved in the case.

Townson told the court that the detectives had repeatedly threatened to hand him over to the British army in the north where, they claimed, he was wanted for three murders. That filled him with fear because he had seen the body of another IRA man killed by the SAS. He believed that if he was dumped back over the border the SAS would also murder him.

He told the court:

> I saw the body of Peter Cleary and he did not have much of a chance as far as I know ... He was shot dead when he was supposed to be running away from the SAS British soldiers. I thought I was going to be shot too ...

Peter Cleary was a staff captain in the Provisional IRA who was

5

shot by an SAS officer while allegedly trying to escape from custody in April 1976. The officer was later identified as Captain Nairac by various witnesses who were with Cleary when he was arrested. They recognised the officer from newspaper pictures after he had been killed.

At Cleary's inquest an officer, identified only as Soldier 'A', said he was a member of the SAS serving at Bessbrook barracks. This was the barracks at which Nairac was then stationed. He had gone with a group of soldiers to arrest Cleary who had resisted. The anonymous officer told the inquest:

> I tackled him round the neck and threw him to the ground, where I frisked him for weapons. Noticing that he was fairly heavy I got hold of him and forced him against the wall of the house. I then took this man by the arm, which I noticed was fairly strong, around the corner to another building.

He then described the series of events leading up to Cleary's death:

> I arrested him saying, 'As a member of Her Majesty's forces, I arrest you', while touching him on the shoulder. I radioed base to request that a helicopter be placed on immediate standby.

The patrol then moved to a nearby field to await the arrival of the helicopter. Cleary was made to lie face down but, on the approach of the helicopter, he was made to stand up. The officer, who was carrying a cocked rifle loaded with eighteen rounds of 7.62mm ball ammunition, said:

> As the Puma started to close in, but before the searchlights were turned on, Cleary hurled himself at me. I was aware of his arms stretched in front of him, directed towards my throat. This was an unprovoked attack.
>
> It was dark, the moon being still obscured by the cloud. I was alone with a known IRA man who had just attempted to escape thirty minutes earlier. I believed him to be a killer who might be heavier and stronger than I was, and who would not hesitate to kill me and make his escape through one of the gaps in the wall and then across

the border, thirty metres away.

As he lunged at me, my instinctive training as an SAS soldier took over. I released the safety catch on my SLR and started shooting, and continued to fire until the danger to my life was past, and that was when Cleary was on the ground. I had no chance to warn him and there had been no time to call out to other members of the patrol.

Claims were made later that the SAS patrol snatched Cleary from a house on the southern side of the border and marched him into the north at gunpoint. Subsequent evidence from Liam Townson himself places him in the vicinity of the shooting around the time of Cleary's death. During his trial for Nairac's murder he told the Special Criminal Court of his reaction to alleged garda threats to dump him across the border:

> The life was scared out of me. I have seen some of the work of the SAS and it is not pleasant. I have seen Peter Cleary shot in the chest when they were finished with him.

Townson told the three judge court, which sat without a jury, that he had been made to stand against a wall for much of the time he was being interviewed and that detectives had pressed down on his shoulders. This went on through the night of his arrest and only ceased when he was taken to a cell at about five o'clock in the morning. He was then unable to sleep because detectives kept rattling a steel bar against the cell door. It was barely daylight, he said, when he was taken back to the interview room where he was questioned by relays of detectives.

Townson told his defence counsel, Mr Patrick MacEntee, SC, that he had been mistreated by five detectives, one of whom had kicked him. He had also been called a 'callous, brutal and murdering bastard'. He added, rather primly:

> I told them that I was not brutal or callous and certainly not a bastard and that I resented the insult to my mother.

7

From the time of his arrest on Saturday until Monday he had been questioned continuously with only a few hours rest, he claimed. Townson denied telling detectives that he was involved in the Nairac killing. He said:

> I was told that I had killed Captain Nairac, that I was taken from the Cabin Bar out to Ravensdale and into a field and that he, Nairac, was supposed to have asked for a priest and that I shot him and left him there.

Later the detectives named in the abuse claim repeatedly denied that Townson suffered any physical assault while being held in Dundalk.

Detective Sergeant Canavan told the court that Townson had told him that Captain Nairac was a great soldier who had told them nothing. On the night of the killing he had been drinking heavily. He asked Nairac who he was and was told 'A Sticky'. Canavan told the court that he understood this to mean a member of the Official IRA.

Later, said Canavan, Townson broke down, crying: 'Why did I do it? I wish I were dead.'

The witness claimed that the accused man then asked for a priest whom he had seen earlier so that he could make a proper confession. He also asked the witness to tell the other gardaí that he was sorry for wasting their time and telling lies.

Townson then allegedly told him:

> I feel much better now that I have told someone. My conscience was killing me. I do not know where the body is. I am not the Officer Commanding. I should never have done it. I walked into it like a lamb.

Canavan told the court that having taken some tablets Townson led gardaí to a field where they found some clothing. In another field they found two guns, one of them the murder weapon, and some ammunition. These were concealed under stones in a ditch.

One of the unusual features of the trial was the appearance of

Townson's solicitor as a defence witness. Mr Donal Carroll, a Dublin lawyer, claimed that he had been repeatedly denied access to Townson at Dundalk Garda barracks. Having been engaged to act for Townson on the night of Sunday, 29 May 1977, he spoke to the duty sergeant at Dundalk by telephone to try to arrange a visit to Townson.

Carroll told the court:

> He told me that some of the gardaí dealing with the case would have to grant the visit, but that none of them was there at that time. I complained that this was highly unusual and that I had never met such an attitude before.

He then asked the sergeant to get one of the relevant gardaí to telephone him when they returned to the barracks. He telephoned again at 10.15 on Monday, but received the same response. He again telephoned at 12.40 and 2.40 pm without gaining satisfaction, so he drove the fifty miles from Dublin to Dundalk, arriving at the barracks at 3.50 pm.

Having asked at the enquiries office to see Townson he was told several times that he would have to wait. As he waited on the steps he was told by a detective that he would be allowed to see Townson at 5 pm. Mr Carroll said he became very annoyed and said he would bring *habeas corpus* proceedings in the High Court the next morning. Having collected Townson's brother Rory, who was waiting in a public house, they returned to the barracks at exactly five o'clock. There they found that Townson had been taken from the barracks to go to Ravensdale Park with gardaí.

He was allowed to see Townson shortly after seven o'clock. The accused man was crying, and holding his head in his hands, said Carroll. At his request the solicitor was left alone in the room with the weeping man. Townson made no response when Carroll told him he was acting as his solicitor. The accused man continued crying as he said:

> I don't want to die. I don't want to die. Please don't give me back to the SAS.

9

The court heard of seven statements allegedly made by Townson, one of them to a detective as they sat in a parked patrol car. Five of these were rejected by the court. The two statements that were admitted amounted to a substantial admission. One of them came after Townson had been visited by his mother, brother and sister. He had been examined by two doctors and had made his confession to a visiting priest.

Mr Justice D'Arcy, presiding, said that Detective Sergeant Canavan told Townson he believed the suspect could assist with garda enquiries into the death of Captain Robert Nairac. Townson said he could not. Townson said that five fellows whom he knew had been charged with this, and that he knew nothing about it.

The judge said:

> Inspector Courtney has given evidence, which we accept, that at this stage the accused was calm and alert and that he made no complaints although requested to do so. The Inspector has further given evidence, which we accept, that no threats were made or inducements offered to the accused.
>
> The accused then asked, 'How long will I get for this?' Guard Canavan said, 'I do not know' and the Inspector said: 'I do not know'. The accused repeated this question a few times and then said: 'I will tell you the truth'.

At this stage, said the judge, Sergeant Canavan cautioned the accused.

> Sergeant Canavan asked the accused if he understood the caution and the accused said he did. Inspector Courtney gave evidence of what was subsequently said. This evidence is supported by that of Sergeant Canavan and we accept it. It is as follows: The accused then said, 'I shot the British captain. He never told us anything. He was a great soldier.
>
> 'I was drinking in Leonard's pub in Dundalk. Danny O'Rourke came in. He told me to get a bit of hardware that there was a job to be done. We went out the road in Kevin Crilly's car ... I got my gun, a .32 revolver. We went to the bridge near the road at Ravensdale. I fired a shot from the gun on the way to test it. They were all there

when I got there, but I don't think young McCoy was there. I had a lot of drink taken.

'I asked the captain who he was and he said, "I am a Stickie". I asked him who he knew and he said Seamus Murphy. I told him I didn't believe him, and he was a British soldier and I had to kill him. I hit him on the head with my fist. I hit him with the butt of my gun also.

'The captain said if you are going to kill me can I have a priest. He was in a bad state. I aimed at his head. I only put one into him. The gun misfired a few times. I left the body there and went home across the fields. I don't know where the body is, and that's the truth.'

Turning to Townson's evidence the judge said:

In his evidence the accused denied that he made the alleged admission ... In his cross-examination the accused denied that he said 'I shot the British captain. He never told us anything. He was a great soldier'. He further denied that he said or made other specific parts of the admission as alleged or deposed to by Detective Inspector Courtney or Detective Sergeant Canavan. We cannot accept the accused's evidence on these points and must reject it.

The judge continued:

In the course of his evidence the accused made various allegations against the guards, in particular against Detective Guard Corrigan, Guards Hynes, Dunne and Godkin and Sergeant Canavan. No useful purpose can be served by setting out these allegations *seriatim* . We do not accept, and consequently reject, the accused's evidence on this matter. We hold that the verbal statement alleged to have been made by the accused to Inspector Courtney and Detective Sergeant Canavan was in fact made by the accused and was a voluntary one.

Townson was the only one of six captured men to be tried in the Republic. The other five men were brought before a court in Belfast the following year. It was the first time anybody had been tried in a British court for an offence committed in the Irish Republic. Gerald Fearon, 21, Thomas Morgan, 18 and Daniel O'Rourke, 33, were all charged with murdering Nairac. Michael McCoy, 22, was accused of kidnapping and Owen Rocks, 22, was accused of withholding information about the kidnapping. Fearon was the only one of the five who was charged with membership of the IRA. He admitted this.

He and Morgan were both sentenced to life. O'Rourke, cleared of murder but convicted of manslaughter, was jailed for ten years. McCoy got five years on the kidnapping charge and Rocks drew a two year sentence. In the absence of a body both trials had one unusual feature since the courts had to make a presumption that Nairac was dead. Despite widespread searches his body has never been found.

All of the men involved in the killing are out of jail now, and one of them, Morgan, is dead, killed in a road accident. The material for this book has come mainly from contemporary records of Nairac's disappearance and the court cases. Much of it has flowed from the memories of various people who were happy to talk, but not happy to be named. In a situation in which the disclosure of awkward and long-buried facts can be fatal their discretion must be respected. To all those who helped I offer my grateful thanks.

Certain passages have been written using a narrative technique. This is to highlight the dramatic intensity of the events they portray. These scenes, including the dialogue, have been reconstructed from the accounts of some of the principals in the Nairac tragedy, as well as from existing documentary evidence and court reports. Where this has occurred italics have been used.

They are there to capture the atmosphere of the times. The dialogue may not be exactly precise and that is understandable. The accounts of these grim events remain clear, but nobody was carrying a tape-recorder on that fatal night.

1

The condemned man lay on the grass in a circle of punishing feet, flinching from the kicks of angry, drunken men. A small river whispered timidly amid the roaring savagery of the night as the man lay there, clutching the hurt to himself. Blood seeped from his broken skin. His face was mottled with bruises, discoloured witnesses to the tattoo of hate that had been beaten upon it.

De Profundis...
Out of the depths I have cried unto thee, O Lord; Lord hear my voice.

He was talking to them now, steady and controlled, saying that they shouldn't let him die without a priest. He was a Catholic, too, he said. If he was to meet God he must first confess his sins. They knew that. They had their Catholic duty. Would they let him go to his death in sin?

His name was Robert Nairac and he was a British army officer who had been caught posing as a man of the people, an amiable extrovert out for a night's enjoyment, a few drinks and a bit of a song. He had adopted a recognisable role as he played the part of the sort of genial fool who buys toleration and acceptance by providing a target for the patronising amusement of others.

That was all a lie, a cover for the old, skulking spy trade. Robert Nairac was a deadly man, capable, cunning and clever, but now he had fallen into the hands of his enemies and there was a price to pay. Treachery has its reckoning and deceit never did come cheap.

Dark hills folded around the night and there was the scent of wild, tender flowers, light and lingering. Defiled grass glowed with spattered blood and the seeping gore nourished the neutral earth as the soldier surrendered his strength in rose-red offerings.

'You can't let me die without a priest,' he said. 'You must get me a priest.'

One of his captors stepped forward: 'I am a priest. You can talk to me.'

That was another lie, tied this time to the appalling blasphemy of a man who had long since discarded the sanctities of his cradle faith.

13

Yet if there was a warning whiff of sulphur in the air that night the vengeful men ignored it. They were not concerned with the bogey-man's hell of eternal torment, the Devil's H-Blocks, the dying embers of a spent mythological terror. Nor were they perturbed by the possibility that the British officer, denied the cleansing sacrament of a last confession, might spend a tormented eternity there. They had a vision of a more immediate and personal hell, an earthbound and political pit in which a paradoxical eternity ended only with succouring death.

The graffiti asked: 'Is there life before death?'

None of them were sure of the answer.

The scene was set for an act of ritual horror, and so a wild and drunken mob of bloodthirsty and vengeful Irishmen, out of control and mad with hate, the manic howls rattling against the walls of their unforgiving skulls, took the British captain from outside a bar in South Armagh and put him to retributive death.

Blasphemy had come again to stalk the land, infecting the countryside with its snarling denial of mercy and compassion. The old constraints turned to vapour while the small decencies that inhibit men, stilling the urgings of their darker longings, withered and died within them. The wolves beneath the skin were running wild and free, stripped of their civilised camouflage, ready to tear and rend in an orgy of conscienceless fury. Stars glimmered faintly in the Neanderthal night, too weak to provide illumination.

If thou, O Lord, shall observe iniquities: Lord, who shall endure it?

The ordeal that was to end in the death of Captain Robert Nairac began after he was taken from the car park of the Three Steps Inn in Drumintee by a gang of unsteady men, most of whom had no connection with the Provisional IRA which was to claim three days after Nairac's disappearance that he had been executed in an official action by the Provisional IRA.

It ended in a field at Ravensdale Park, County Louth on the banks of the small River Flurry. The death scene lies just south of where the main road linking Belfast and Dublin crosses the border into the Irish Republic. A network of roads lead down from the hilly terrain of South Armagh to link with the main trunk road. For drivers familiar with the back roads the travelling time between the Three Steps and Ravensdale Park, a wooded and secluded residential area, is less than fifteen minutes.

Later, at one of the trials that followed Nairac's death, a witness said:

> I saw a lot of the boys kicking the SAS man and pulling him by the hair. The SAS man was put into the back of a car. He was forced into the car and a gun stuck into his back.

The Cortina car and its passengers lurched off into the night, part of a drunken convoy of death. Later estimates put at least thirteen people in the vengeance gang, and various sources confirmed that most of them had been drinking heavily. When the cars reached the small humpback bridge at Ravensdale Park the battered soldier was pulled out and frog-marched into a field which runs below the bridge. He was pushed down behind a wall.

Nairac was partly lying with his back and head resting on the dry stone wall. He was covering his face with his hands to protect it from more blows, and blood was seeping from his mouth and nose. One of the captors was down on one knee beside the soldier, pushing him for information. Others joined in the interrogation, a Greek chorus, slurred of speech, bursting with physical malevolence.

'What's your name, you bastard?'

There was the dull slap of abusive knuckles pounding on skin and bone, mulching the small capillary arteries so that the flesh shone green and brown and blue where they had burst. Then the gore started at the point where the skin actually split.

'You're an SAS man, aren't you?'

A sudden foot snaked out from the forest of legs, slamming into the ribs and sending new waves of pain radiating through the bruised torso. Now the pain surged through him in rippling layers as successive blows started the old waves of numbing agony surging anew. Each fresh assault intensified the pain until it became the focal point of his life, the only reality.

My soul hath relied on his word: my soul hath hoped in the Lord.

15

Nairac told them then that he was a Sticky, a member of the Official IRA who were lately locked in a bitter feud with their Provisional counterparts. The Officials got their nick-name because of their preference for using adhesive backing for the paper Easter lilies with which they commemorated the 1916 Rising. The Provisionals used pins.

'I'm Danny McErlean and I'm in the Officials,' he said.

He was speaking with the near Belfast accent he had picked up while working on English building sites, breathing in the essence of the displaced Irish urban peasant, burrowing into the alehouse republicanism of the God-forsaken army of jobless men who cross the sea to heave a shovel for Wimpey or carry a hod for Mac-Alpine.

Nairac had done that as part of his training for an intelligence role in the north, quietly absorbing the petty details of Irish life as he shared a maudlin pint with homesick emigrants in some north London bar, filing away the information he would later drop with studied casualness, claiming it as part of his own life experience.

The craic was good in Cricklewood, so he moved like a sly imperial fox among the exiled Paddies, keeping the cover story wide and flexible and never allowing anybody to pin it down to specifics. Rosy nights of lies and laughter, viewed through the distorting prism of a pint glass bottom. Whatever. It all added up for Captain Robert Nairac of the Grenadier Guards, an Oxford graduate on secondment to the SAS, to the making of some class of dubious Irishman.

'You can check who I am on here,' he said, calling out a Belfast telephone number to his tormentors.

One of the men wrote down the number on a cigarette packet and put it in his pocket. Nobody was going to make that call. Nobody was that anxious to flirt with danger.

They knew enough to understand that it was possibly a last-ditch military alarm line. The very act of dialling the number and asking about Danny McErlean would alert the military to the fact that Nairac, whose code name would be recognised, was in deep trouble and trigger an immediate automatic trace. Then, while the operator on the other end stalled the caller with a well-rehearsed routine, police and troops would be swooping down to make the capture.

Suddenly the soldier, pulling together the last remaining reserves of his strength, leapt to his feet and tried to make a run for it. He moved slowly, groggy from the beating he had taken, rubber legs buckling beneath him. There were enough of them around to hold him.

Young Tom, seventeen years old and eager for the fray, was one of the first to try to restrain the struggling officer. He said later: 'He managed to get to his feet; he began to struggle and during the struggle I hit him a kick in the balls.'

So the tragi-comedy lurched on towards its soiled, indecent, end as the British officer, trained in the terrible arts of human destruction, lay still beneath the random kicks of a beardless, beery boy who had recently discovered that patriotism may be well expressed with the toe of a shoe. Nairac was on his back, looking up at the sky while the wall of convulsive violence rose solidly around him.

'I want a priest,' he whispered. 'Get me a priest.'

The men in the field did not want a priest; they wanted a hitman. Young Tom, hovering around the captured man, high on the excitement of it all, recalled: 'I heard Terry tell Kevin to go and get Townson or some of the boys. I knew he was talking about Liam Townson from Meigh who is in the Provies and who is on the run.'

Liam Townson, drunk in Dundalk after an all-day session, was being brought in as the official executioner. Once he fired the shot the killing became a Provisional IRA job. The times were wild and dangerous and it was well to cover a lethal action with some degree of apparent legitimacy. The men in the field were drunk, but they all knew the difference between one soldier shooting another and taking a man's life as the culmination of some Bacchanalian revel.

THE MURDEROUS MEN in the field were living at the fag-end of Britain's old imperial aberration and now, in their sodden brutality, they were adding another death to the long, lethal pageant of horror that had seen their country brought under alien rule by sword and crossbow, rifle, bayonet and hangman's noose. In that sense Captain Nairac lost his life in expiation of centuries of bloodied oppression. Less fancifully, he died because he had chosen to help impose the continuance of a worn-out and discredited regime upon an angry and militantly resentful people.

His captors and their kin had spent an age flinching beneath the aggressive racism of a self-proclaimed master caste, living out their days under the enforced tutelage of an Orange ascendancy which had, by guile and armed force, managed to continue Catholic political serfdom into the late twentieth century.

The system developed its own hierarchies, with members of the possessing classes also featuring as the leaders of the various loyalist institutions which served to bolster both their economic and political power. They were sleek, self-satisfied men, these anointed of the Lord, and if they appeared to have as much fervent regard for King William of Orange as they did for the Deity that may have been because the Almighty has never actually defeated a Catholic army in the field.

Armed with Bible and blunderbuss, the ancestors of this tribe arrived in Ireland during the seventeenth century, lured by the promise of land held out by a conquering Britain which dreamt of swamping the Catholic and rebellious natives beneath a flood of Calvinistic Scots and their English counterparts.

The settlers, adherents of some of the wilder religious perversions dreamed up by men of bilious temperament and inferior intellect in the wake of Martin Luther's righteous challenge to a spiritually decayed age, brought with them a grossly impertinent belief in their own inherent superiority. This arrogant and illogical notion continues to be consciously nurtured by their descendants despite the mighty weight of evidence against it.

Even where religious fervour retreats before the onslaught of contemporary neo-paganism the idea is kept alive for the political advantages it yields. When a dynamic and non-sectarian civil rights movement rose in the late 1960s to challenge the inevitable abuses which arose as the result of such supremacist thinking the suddenly embattled Protestants reacted with brutal fury.

In the ensuing flare-up loyalist power wavered. The Royal Ulster Constabulary along with its sectarian B Special auxiliaries were seen to be facing defeat at the hands of insurrectionist Catholics after a series of pitched battles in Derry, so the British army was ordered in. That was in late 1969.

The soldiers, it was said, had come to keep the peace, but in doing that they were also protecting Britain's inexplicable interest in a cluster of green and pleasant Irish counties. They were also effectively shoring up the waning power of the north's sectarian ruling class. Fifty years after the enforced partition of Ireland the bills were beginning to come in.

The act of partition was largely brought about under the pressure of blackmail. At a time when Britain was prepared to concede self-government to a newly autonomous Irish nation she found herself faced with a threatened army mutiny and a promised revolt by the armed Protestants of the north if they were placed under Dublin's sovereignty. That set the standard for the Ulster Protestants' vaunted loyalty to Britain which has always been conditional on the British government doing precisely what was required of it.

It is commonplace now to talk about the gerrymandered electoral boundaries, the lies that were told and the promises that were made and broken, and it would be tedious were it not for the fact that the Catholic population of the six occupied counties of the north are still paying the price for this masterly exercise in cynical manipulation.

What is both surprising and demeaning is that many years after these events Britain is still prepared to use her soldiers to maintain a political situation which totally lacks any claim to moral validity since it was fabricated under duress. Nor can the pragmatic argument that Britain regards the area as having strategic and economic importance be sustained.

Equally puzzling has been the muted response of members of Dáil Éireann, many of whom appear to have slept through the rampant period of Irish history which began in 1969 with a modulated call for justice. It turned raucous only when answered by the strident violence of a caste of vengeful and implacable overlords.

Confronted with the warlike militancy of Orange fascism within an area over which the Dáil claimed jurisdiction, these laggardly personages have been notably slow in demanding that the situation be remedied, and remedied with the utmost swiftness. They had a legitimate case to make; it is surprising that they did not pursue it vociferously and unequivocally with the British government whose only claim to the six counties rests on a dubious right of conquest. Nor did these tawdry political time-servers take the opportunity to state the case for Irish reunification upon the various international platforms that were open to them.

As the increasing savagery of the northern situation continued to spawn greater brutalities this sad collection of pusillanimous poltroons took evasive action by putting on the mantle of the professional craw thumper. Clad in this protective garb they then entrenched themselves behind a barricade of specious moralistics from where they condemned republican violence while largely ignoring its causes. It was a retreat into the sort of blanched cowardice which is known in political circles as pragmatic realism.

There were some honourable exceptions. Having made their position known these were mostly to be found shuffling around the wastelands, mining the salt as they serve out some Irish equivalent of Siberian banishment.

In the absence of any movement for change by the established politicians the north erupted in sudden violence. It had taken almost fifty years for the explosion to happen, but it had always been inevitable. It was a time of pogroms, with Catholics being burned out of their homes by rampaging Protestant mobs. The Catholics retaliated by setting fire to Protestant houses.

The British army did succeed in curbing the wilder excesses of the warring clans, but armies are not trained to fulfil the role of peacemaker. Inevitably the soldiers started shooting and, equally inevitably, most of their fire was directed at the Catholics who were the ones who wanted them to go home and stay home. The Irish Republican Army, dormant since the late 1950s, stirred from its sleep and went off in search of arms. As the opposing guns pointed at each other the Circus of Death arrived in town and settled in for a long run.

It was against this background of bloody disintegration that Captain Nairac was either murdered or executed, depending on the point of view. There was a fatal symmetry surrounding his death which dictated the outcome of events. In the classic tradition of tragedy, there is a sense in which the victim is also the prime mover, the one whose actions make inevitable the ultimate act of self-wrought destruction.

By his own active compliance in undercover activities, which relied upon concealing his military role, Nairac helped create the climate in which it was possible for his killers to believe that his death was no more than a mechanical and neutral act of insurrectionary warfare. He was a spy and everybody shoots spies, don't they? In that sense he shared some of the responsibility for his own execution.

Nairac paid with his life and the men who killed him also paid a penalty when they exchanged their humanity for the degrading blood-fury that brought about his brutalised end. Six of them also went to jail, so some sort of justice, austere and inexact, was once again done in a landscape where the very trees call out for some small gift of mercy. Another casual act of corrosive indecency had been added to the litany of guilt and suffering that had thrummed its malign melody down the stricken years.

AT 21.25 HOURS on Saturday 14 May 1977 Captain Robert Nairac, dressed in flared jeans, anorak and workman's boots, booked out of the army barracks at Bessbrook Mill in the small County Armagh village from which the mill took its name. His hair was long and shaggy and he wore a moustache. Nairac, described by one of his former colleagues as looking 'like a displaced hippy' was clearly at the start of what the duty officer recognised as yet another mystery mission.

Nairac was tall, tough, twenty-nine years old, a fighter whose nose had been flattened in his days at Oxford, when he was resurrecting the university boxing team. He was both hard and sensitive, a Renaissance man born out of time, the soldier-scholar slipping uneasily into a clanking world where poetry comes with chamfered edges and the modern elegies have machine-tooled joints.

Nairac provided some sort of sweaty, physical leadership to the pugilists at his university, even as his mind did an elegant glissade across the academic curriculum. He left Oxford with a history degree having already successfully passed through the Royal Milit-

ary Academy at Sandhurst, one of the world's great officer fact-
ories.

There are nine hundred landscaped acres of Sandhurst set
along the border between Surrey and Berkshire, two of Britain's
most affluent counties. The area around is studded with lakes and
woodland. It is an arcadian setting for a meltdown mixture of
building styles that range from the neo-classical elegance of the
main building to the leprous rash of Nissen huts which litter the
grounds like an outbreak of architectural acne.

Training at Sandhurst was largely about turning unformed
young men into the leaders of an army which draws enormous
strengths from its long centuries of unbroken tradition. In defer-
ence to a changing world Nairac's training also included courses
which taught how to fight in a built-up area and how to deal with
riots. There was also a course which taught the young officer
cadets how to behave themselves in polite society.

Anthony Beevor, a former army officer, recalls in his book
Inside the British Army the retired major general who regretted the
changing times with the remark:

> When I went to Sandhurst we were not taught to behave like gentle-
> men, because it never occurred to anyone that we should behave
> otherwise.

Commenting on these lessons in behaviour and etiquette Beevor
remarks:

> The Guards and cavalry clique among the cadets may still raise their
> eyebrows in amusement at the earnest note-taking around them, but
> this shrink-wrapping of social codes into 'training packages' seems to
> symbolise not the preservation of the world known to previous
> generations, but its final passing.

It is unlikely that Nairac would have joined in any guying of the
social inadequacies of potential officers since he certainly possessed the sort of courteous self-assurance that never sullies itself
by displays of petty snobbery. Captain Tony Clarke, who joined

the Parachute Regiment as a ranker wrote a gritty book *Contact* about his two tours of duty in the north. In the book he recalls meeting Nairac who had arrived in 1974 as part of a Grenadier Guards company which was to take over North Belfast from the Paras:

> The officer commanding comes in with the Grenadier Guards advance party to introduce me. 'Tony, this is Bob Nairac who will be assigned to you for the hand-over period.' I shake hands with a stocky guy with curly black hair, far removed from the normal type of Guards officer you usually meet. I take in the broken nose and cheerful grin and think 'Thank God I haven't got one of those guys with a mouth full of marbles'.

Nairac had joined the Grenadier Guards from Sandhurst. This was a regiment which marched proudly out of a gloried past carrying its sustaining burden of tradition with a swaggering ease that mocked the pretensions of other, lesser, formations. It was from this haven of foot drill spectaculars and languid social graces that he was seconded for a tour with the SAS in the north.

That had been a cloak-and-dagger experience, Bulldog Drummond meets the Fenian hordes, the stuff of boyhood daydreams and never mind about the dead bodies. Now he was back, running with the spooks this time, operating in the fertile ground where military intelligence meets the clinically efficient killers of the Special Air Service. Few people knew quite where Captain Nairac fitted in, but everybody knew that it was somewhere dark and dangerous. Military prudence dictated that it was better not to ask for the details.

The operations officer on the night that Nairac disappeared was Captain David Alan Collett. He booked Nairac out of the mill and noted that he intended operating in the South Armagh area nicknamed the Murder Triangle. It had been given that name by an embattled military who treated it with the caution due to a proven IRA stronghold. Collett watched as the undercover officer walked out to his red Triumph Dolomite car, registration number CIB 4253. The car had been issued to Nairac by the army and its num-

ber plates were changed every week to guard against the danger of
identification by the IRA. It was equipped with a disguised military radio. The wireless also had a hidden panic button to be pressed for assistance in case of extreme danger.

For an undercover operator working in the danger zone of
South Armagh, wild Injun territory in which every hedge-row
might conceal a Fenian war party, the car provided both a life support system and an umbilical link to the stand-by unit that was in
continual readiness for an emergency call-out. Nairac headed out
through the massive steel gates to disappear into the Apache bad-
lands, out into the Comanche hills, down into the Sioux valley, the
Lone Ranger thrusting into the darkness of the menacing night. Hi-
ho, Silver!

This was an area retained for Britain only by the bristling presence of a saturation military force, obliged to operate from fortified heights by the rampages of the disaffected natives. In time the
soldiers learned to move everything, including their camp rubbish,
by helicopter. They did that because of the danger of ambush by
IRA attackers, lurking at the roadside with bombs and bullets.

It was a land of fantasy and pretence, a proving ground for the
sort of multi-purpose adolescent myth that comes wrapped in the
fevered imaginings of men whose rationalisations owed more to
the naked knuckle than to the mind.

Captain Collett was the last Briton to see Nairac alive. He did
hear from Nairac again, though. There was one routine radio check
call at 21.58 hours. After that, only silence.

*THE BAR WAS steaming with the close-packed mass of border cow-
boys, there for a Saturday night blast of Grand Ol' Opry, Armagh
style. A shadowing sun slid down the May sky and the memory of the
day's heat wrapped itself warmly around the long, white-walled
bungalow bar. The fresh-faced country boy at the microphone,
transformed now into a rambunctious ranch hand, twanged his geet-
ar and belted out a song about love's desolation and the heartbreak
to be got from a honky tonk woman.*

The men slugged at their pints and nodded contentedly, gazing

24

*around the room in beery-eyed appraisal of the local honky tonks.
Another sort of imperialism was at work here, welcomed and invited
in without resistance, as one by one the hamlets and towns of rural
Ireland surrendered to the rhythmic rawness of American country
and western music. Culchie and Western the wiseheads called it, a
wordplay on rural simplicities.*

*Nairac glanced around the smoky room as he shouldered his
way through the press of drinkers, pushing to the bar and calling for
a pint of stout. There were more than two hundred people crowded
into the room, many of them strangers. The Three Steps Inn near the
flyspeck village of Drumintee had become a favoured Saturday night
haunt for the younger set who drove the few miles from Newry town
for an evening's entertainment.*

*They came to mix in easy camaraderie with the local fugitives
from field and farm. The singer at the microphone wandered down
the Streets of Laredo, sashaying into a lyrical showdown with the
Man from Laramie before he finally perished as the last casualty of
the Gunfight at the OK Corral. Nairac took a pull at his drink and
started up a conversation with a grey haired, sixtyish man who stood
at his elbow. The man said a drop of rain would do the crops no
harm, although we could hold on for a day or two yet and where
would you be from yourself? Nairac shrugged off the inquisition and
slipped into a rehearsed lie.*

*Desmond McCreesh, the landlord of the Three Steps Inn was in
the car park when the British officer arrived. McCreesh had his own
security methods. He kept watch on the car park, ready to turn away
the rowdies before they had the chance to get a taste of drink, or even
the smell of it. He saw Nairac's red Toledo pull in at about 10.15 and
watched as the driver locked the car and walked into the bar.*

*Inside the bar the long, nourishing pints were working their
anaesthetic magic on the assembled male drinkers while the mellow-
ing honky-tonk women chattered happily over their short and fashionable drinks. Nairac was part of a group of men, joining in the
general conversation and buying a round of drinks.*

One of the men asked: 'Where was it you said you were from?'

'Belfast,' Nairac said.

'What part?'

'I'm from Ardoyne,' he said.

25

'You have it rough up there, what with the Brits and the peelers and the bloody Orangies and all.'

'Rough enough,' Nairac said. *'Aye, rough enough, but what's the use of talking? There's no end to it.'*

Nairac pushed his way through the crowded bar to the toilet, stopping on his way back to talk to Seán Murphy, a member of the band who was also acting as compere.

'Can a Belfast man sing a song?' he asked.

'I told him to write it down on a piece of paper,' Murphy recalled, 'but he told me just to call it out. He spoke with a Belfast accent and gave his name as Danny McErlean. He came up and sang two republican songs. One was "The Broad Black Brimmer" and I'm not sure what the other song was.'

The other song was 'The Boys of the Old Brigade,' a celebration of the IRA's role in freeing the twenty-six counties of the Irish Republic of the British presence. The broad black brimmer was the preferred headgear of some IRA volunteers on active service during the turbulent years that followed the 1916 Rising.

Murphy recalled: 'This man was able to tell me what key he wanted. He was quite a good singer. When he finished singing he went back to the bar and rejoined the people he was with.'

The musician was to have one more encounter with the undercover soldier that night.

'We finished playing at about 11.35 pm and started to pack up. I know this man was still in the bar because when I was taking off my guitar I accidentally hit him on the head with it. I remember apologising to him.'

Things started to go badly wrong for Nairac some time before that. While he was up at the microphone, giving a baritone rendition of his two songs, one of the men at the bar said: 'That's the strangest Belfast accent I've ever heard.'

Another man nodded in agreement. 'He says he's been working away in Canada and that his name's McErlean. You know what McErlean is, don't you? It's the name of a bloody bakery.'

The man smiled: 'Maybe he got his name off the side of a loaf. There's a well-known member of the Official IRA with that name, too. I think we should ask that boy a few questions.'

Not long after the chance blow from the musician Nairac left the bar followed by two men who were to take him to a rendezvous with death. After they had spoken to him he walked out of the bar ahead of the two men. He was a man prepared to walk into danger, possibly because he reasoned he had a better chance of dealing with any threat in the open than in a bar packed with republican sympathisers in various stages of sobriety. As they moved towards the door two teenage youths moved ahead of them. They had been told to scout the roads, making sure there were no army patrols around.

There may have been another reason why Nairac walked so willingly towards his death. It is possible that he believed that the men who had followed him from the bar posed no danger. Desmond McCreesh, 43 years old at the time, was still in the car park as the men left. After police had roused McCreesh out of bed at seven o'clock the next morning he recognised the driver of the red Toledo from a photograph they showed him. It was Nairac, he said. He did not know the man's name until police told him, but that is who it was. He had watched the missing army officer leaving the bar the previous night.

He told the police: 'At around 11.30 pm I saw three people go up past my car to the top of the car park ... As they walked past my view the soldier was slightly in front of the other two, a couple of feet or so.'

Looking back on it seventeen years later he recalled: 'I didn't see everything that was going on because I was on my way into the bar when I saw them. I got the name of running a Provo pub and I tried to sue the *Daily Express* newspaper for saying that, but I was not strong enough. People just stopped coming. The whole affair nearly put me out of business.'

After the IRA claimed it had executed Nairac the army was to disclose that he had also been in the Three Steps Inn on the Friday night before his disappearance. Speculation mounted that Nairac, who had a reputation for never making a move without a thought-out purpose, was there to make contact with some new source. He was believed to have recruited informers in the Forkhill area, just a few miles from the Three Steps Inn. A military colleague, supporting this view, said: 'He was a tough, professional soldier who left nothing to chance.'

Yet that could not be wholly true. For some time before his death Nairac had been carrying out his activities with an extraordinary lack of regard for his own personal safety. In Crossmaglen, heartland of the Provisional IRA in South Armagh, he was known in the bars as Danny Boy, because of his fondness for entertaining the local drinkers with that song.

On the night of his disappearance he breached security by not maintaining radio contact with his base. By the time a search had been mounted for him at 1 am on the Sunday morning he was in an isolated field across the Irish border, pleading for a priest as the certainty of imminent death gripped him.

Years have been spent trying to establish some rational pattern that might explain his obvious carelessness. The theory given the greatest weight is that on the night of his death Nairac was trying to make contact with a new source whom he had not met, and was therefore unable to recognise. Since neither he nor the new recruit would have known each other some sort of signal was necessary. In that jostling bar, hazy with cigarette smoke and so crowded that it would have been almost impossible to establish direct contact with a stranger, the possibility of singing a pre-arranged song at the microphone offered the perfect opportunity for Nairac to reveal himself.

The assumption then is that he must have believed the men who followed him from the bar posed no threat to his safety and were there merely to become part of the tainted little network of collaborators that Nairac and his colleagues were so assiduously building. It is also possible that Nairac believed himself to be immune from attack.

Yet he was in immediate danger and the proof of that came when one of the men following him to the red Toledo car paused to put a scarf around his face before sprinting across to where Nairac stood opening his car.

The group had stopped playing in the bar, but the sound of boozy voices, muffled by liquor, swept fuzzily over the car park, delivering some maudlin, mawkish, tailend-of-the-evening pub song. There was a shout of laughter, a voice calling for order, the tinkle of collected glasses. Somebody was closing down the evening, putting it away until tomorrow. Nairac breathed in the night air. It was gentle and caressing, scented with sweet grasses.

There was a sudden noise and Nairac turned to see a man whose face was covered by a scarf rushing at him. Before he could react the man was on him, grappling him to the ground as other men came running up to kick at him. As the attackers tried to pin him flat to the ground Nairac reached in to his shoulder holster, pulling out the specially adapted 9mm Browning pistol with its featherweight, elongated trigger. He tried to level it but there were four or five men around him and one of them kicked the gun out of his hand.

The pistol skidded away out of sight under the car and the man who was straddling his body leaned over and began groping for it. All the men were on Nairac now, beating him and holding him down. The main attacker scrabbled around in the darkness until he found the pistol. Then he put it to Nairac's head.

'Don't move, you fucker,' he said. 'Don't move or I'll shoot you.'

BY THE EARLY hours of the morning the army knew that something had gone badly wrong. Nairac had been due to make a check call at 11.30 to let the Operations Officer know that everything was all right. He never did make the call. Captain David Collett fretted about the missing communication for more than half an hour, wondering whether Nairac was in trouble or whether he was with a source, or in some situation where he could not break cover. Whatever the reason, it was a grave breach of security procedures.

Collett nursed his growing sense of unease for thirty-five minutes and then picked up the telephone to inform the commanding officer that they had either a missing or negligent officer on their hands. It was five minutes after midnight on a moonless Sunday morning. A few pinpoint stars gleamed across immeasurable space, but the night was impenetrably dark. That ruled out the chance of any major search before daybreak.

There were some things that could be done, though. Off-duty SAS men were pulled out of their beds or away from their drinks in the mess and sent on a series of scouting missions around the countryside. The officer organising the search realised that little help could be expected from the cap-badge army, the one in uniform, at that time of night. Mostly they would be back in their camps, but there might be a few Paras or other special units out on hidden stake-outs.

He gave orders that all military units should be alerted to the fact that undercover soldiers were quartering the countryside, armed and dressed as civilians. It would not do for somebody to mistake them for Boyos and open up on them. At some stage the Royal Ulster Constabulary might have to be told, but not yet. Better wait to see if the missing captain turned up.

Somebody contacted the garda síochána, asking for a tight watch on traffic moving south across the border but, by the time the republic's police received this request the gory little drama was nearing its grisly climax. On the northern side extra staff were brought into the Operations Room as the emergency widened and moved upward, turning into a pyramid of concern with the senior men at the top straddling their own apex of anxiety.

One man tracked the mobile SAS units on a large wall map as they radioed in to report on the country they had covered. They drove slowly through the night, signalling in at short and regular intervals. Everybody waited for the sighting or the suspicion that would lead them to the missing officer, but it did not come.

'There's nothing moving out here,' one of the patrols reported. 'There's only rabbits.'

'After you with the rabbits,' the radio man said.

It was an old soldiers' joke, an obscene reference to the supposedly unappeasable and brutishly unselective sexual appetites of the military.

'You wouldn't know whether to cook them or ...'

'I'd know all right. Keep looking. He's out there somewhere and we've got to get to him fast.'

Tension mounted through the night and by first light every army unit in South Armagh had been stood-to as the military commanders completed their plans for a detailed ground search of the area. As the sky lightened a succession of armoured personnel carriers nosed warily out into the hostile hills. They moved like questing insects, beetling forward with a blind and implacable purpose.

Countryside sounds broke into the day; the complaining voices of hard-done-by cattle; the boastful challenges of farmyard cocks; the joyful chorus of awakening birds. These sounds printed themselves on the lightening sky, a pastoral counterpoint to the thin, mechanical whine of the questing army saracens. Nobody told the Royal Ulster Constabulary about the missing officer until 5.45 am and when they did a senior policemen said: 'Lost an officer, have you? Now that was a bit careless.'

It was the sort of needling crack that the army expected and it went part way to explaining why the military had not called on the police until their help became absolutely vital. By now Nairac had been missing for more than seven hours. Anxious men controlling the search had long given up the notion that Nairac was merely playing the maverick, ignoring routine out of arrogance, apathy, stupidity or indifference. Nobody stayed out of contact that long unless he was under physical restraint or dead. The commonly held view was that Nairac was either one or the other.

Within an hour of being called in the police had found Nairac's car at the Three Steps Inn. The windscreen had been smashed and a door handle torn off. There was blood on the ground near the car. All the signs pointed to a desperate struggle having occurred. It fitted in with what everyone knew of Nairac. If he had been waylaid he would not have gone quietly.

By now the South Armagh border area was swarming with military and police. With a focal point provided by the discovery of the car the search radiated out to take in Forkhill, Crossmaglen, Drumintee and other small settlements that lay within easy distance of the public house. Bemused farmers suddenly found their homes surrounded by heavily armed soldiers, intent on searching both the buildings and the land. Garda were carrying out the same operation on the other side of the border, peering into thickets, probing the corners of barns, asking questions about some missing British soldier. The probings created more alarm than information. Nobody had seen or heard anything.

There were people about, though, who did know something. They were members of the kidnap gang. Almost twenty years after the event one of them recalled: 'A patrol of soldiers went past as we were beating Nairac in the car park. We were scuffling around and making quite a lot of noise. They just walked on, not stopping to see what was happening. I suppose they thought it was just a bunch of drunken Paddies beating the heads off each other.'

As the search went on Brigadier David Woodford, commander of the 3rd Infantry Brigade which covered the entire border area, denied Nairac was a member of the SAS but said he had dealings with the unit and served with it on occasion. For sceptics who knew the SAS tactic of hiding behind a permanent smokescreen the brigadier's protestations seemed a little disingenuous. Not even senior British officers get told all the facts where the SAS is concerned.

Brigadier Woodford said:

> He was very well known in these parts by the army, the RUC and the local people. What went wrong on this occasion is something we are trying to find out. If it turns out that we have lost this man I will be deeply saddened.

The time of uncertainty came to an end three days after Nairac's disappearance when the IRA said its members had killed him. A statement issued by the 1st Battalion IRA, South Armagh, said:

> We arrested him on Saturday night and executed him after interrogation in which he admitted he was an SAS man. Our intelligence officers had a number of photographs in their possession and the late captain had been recognised from them.

That statement confirmed the army's fears and quashed any hopes of finding the missing officer alive. It also added a furious urgency to the need to recover his body to offset the propaganda advantage the IRA had gained. That was the reasoning of the plain and practical men whose task now was to minimise the damage caused by Nairac's abduction and death. The search was stepped up with hundreds of police and troops moved in to search the area.

Their efforts drew support from Father Denis Faul, a priest in

Dungannon, County Tyrone, who was shocked by the disappearance of the body and the consequent denial of a proper burial. Down the years this schoolmaster-priest earned himself a reputation for the uncompromising vigour with which he attacked those whose conduct fell short of the Christian ideal. Both the Provisional IRA and the British army were the frequent focus of his righteous wrath, as were the police and politicians of all persuasions. The single unifying theme running through all his critical pleadings was the one that urges a duty of loving compassion towards other God-created humans. He demanded that the body be produced immediately, saying that if it was not then it could only be assumed that the dead captain had been badly beaten while alive.

It was a suitable time for the ghouls to crawl out of the black fastnesses of their own fevered imaginings. Police switchboards were jammed with calls from people claiming to know the whereabouts of the missing corpse. Some demanded money for the information. One particular tip-off sounded feasible. It came from a man who claimed to have seen a group of men dumping a body in a quarry. The man said he had been parked in the quarry with his girlfriend. A major search of the quarry was called off after three days when the call was discovered to have been yet another tasteless hoax.

Nobody has yet produced the body, and suggestions about its whereabouts range from the stomach-churning theory that it was fed through the mincing machinery of a meat factory to the more likely explanation that it was thrown down a boghole in the mountainous region that separates South Armagh from County Louth. In the absence of a body six men were jailed for offences connected with Nairac's death, but the lack of a corpse did not leave a complete blank. There are enough memories of the dead man still floating around to build up a picture of a complex and contradictory individual.

Brigadier Woodford had a brisk, soldierly view. He said:

He was one man, a very brave man out of a number of very brave men, who have been trying to deal with terrorism.

33

Nairac's sister Rosemond, thirty-six at the time of his death, reinforced that view. She said:

> He died doing what he felt and stated to be his duty.

Others detected a yearning restlessness, combined with a need to make some sort of point about courage and manhood. One or two detected the sort of hubristic insolence that invites destruction. One of Nairac's teachers spoke to Martin Dillon, author of *The Dirty War*. Dillon records that he said:

> I always expected him to come to a sad end because I always saw a sad end to his nature.

From an Oxford contemporary, Duncan Fallowell, came claims that Nairac joined in drug taking parties and threw a tantrum when he found Fallowell in bed 'with his favourite boxing Blue'. Fallowell has written *Days in the Life*, a book of Oxford reminiscences, in which he says Nairac 'might have liked to be gay'. After the boxing Blue incident, he claims, Nairac wanted to take LSD, the mind-altering lysergic acid drug.

Running alongside that are the persistent rumours from various quarters that the ultra-masculine Nairac was a man who battled against homosexual leanings. At times their pull was too strong for him and his resistance crumbled, they say. In at least one case, according to one man who was close to both parties, that resulted in a passionately committed gay affair which was still going on at the time of Nairac's death.

There is yet another perception of Robert Nairac and it comes from Major Fred Holroyd who knew him while serving as a Military Intelligence Officer in the north. Major Holroyd was an ambitious soldier whose career got bruised to destruction after he was caught in the middle of a territorial battle between Britain's two spook services, MI5 and MI6. Holroyd remembers Nairac as being brave and keen if a little rash. That, he says, was the face of Captain Nairac that everybody saw.

There are, though, strong claims that another face existed, the dark and secret face of a cold and conscienceless murderer. The evidence supporting this comes from a boast Nairac made to Holroyd that he had crossed the border to assassinate an IRA fugitive. He backed this claim with a photograph of the victim lying dead in his own blood.

There are also claims from members of loyalist hit squads, set up and armed by the military and then turned loose to murder Catholics, that Captain Nairac was their briefing officer. A gun used in the Miami Showband Massacre in which a gang of loyalists dressed in British army uniform killed three Catholic musicians has been linked to Nairac. One of the survivors of the massacre says he heard an English voice giving orders. The suggestion has been floated that the voice belonged to Nairac.

The shutters have been down for years as the subtle mandarins who guard Britain's secrets maintain an impregnable silence about matters surrounding the death of Robert Nairac, bit player and victim of their country's Irish tragedy. They do not speak because they know that in some circumstances silence is the only possible answer.

2

A blanketing drabness lay across Britain in the year that Robert Nairac was born. The Second World War had been over for just three years and the unhealed scars of that total and merciless conflict still festered on the land. Bomb sites and the rubbled memory of air attacks littered the major cities, dusty laments to a broken and flattened landscape. There were queues at the shops as housewives waited patiently for the small quantities of meat, butter and cheese that was their rationed due.

Life was still being lived as an exercise in survival and there was little time for grace. It was a washed-out age, dismal and depleted: somebody had taken all the colours of the world and made a funeral pyre of them. A weak and wounded country lay torpid in convalescence, knowing that recovery would be long, slow and painful, and possibly never quite complete.

In that year, 1948, England, along with much of the rest of Europe, looked like a secondhand country, jaded and shabby, a cast-off nation mantled in the ragged remnants of old, half-remembered glories. Weary, ill-clad people roved the austere streets trailing a resigned and apathetic acceptance of their place in a shoddy world. Nobody had told them that the cost of war continues to be met by its survivors, but then nobody had ever told them anything much. They were the remnants of the dole queue generation of the hungry 1930s. Very early on they had learned that their role in life was simply to endure.

For some this meant the adoption of a near brutish fatalism that absolved them from the need for either protest or discontent. That was an attitude which was to become briefly unpopular. After the war a big majority took another road, voting for an illusory promise of permanent social change by bringing in a Labour government which wore the bright, shining armour of righteous rejection. That was another hallucination, of course, another surrender to the magic of tricks that are done with mirrors.

Before long the armour lost its gleam, becoming tarnished by the shoddy compromises which politicians make when idealism proves to be a barrier to the immediate needs of a self-serving and egocentric reality. The joyless and largely unrealised disillusion which stalked the streets of post-war Britain resumed its sullen pacing.

It was into this world of shrinking opportunity and diminishing prestige that Robert Nairac was born. He was one of four children bred from a Protestant mother and a Catholic father. In later years, some said, this religiously mixed family background, which was both smooth and uncomplicated, was to fuel the incredulity with which he viewed the Northern Irish situation.

That is difficult to believe. It is unlikely that Nairac would have made a connection between his privileged home, a warm and loving haven where differences were welcomed as a manifestation of individuality, and the fuelled sectarianism he met in the north. Nairac was born into the patrician Catholicism of England's privileged classes, a group which often finds more in common with their non-Catholic peers than with socially inferior co-religionists. He knew nothing of marching men beating lambeg drums and bawling out their triumphalist anthems until he met them in the north.

One commentator, Malcolm Stuart, said at the time of his death:

> Robert went to Ampleforth College in North Yorkshire, the Eton of the upper class Catholics; people who, for the most part, are the descendants of those who secretly passed down their faith through the Reformation.
>
> If they have a weakness, it is that they are resentful of the domination of Catholics of Irish descent in present day Britain. There are few sympathisers of the IRA among the Catholics who send their sons to Ampleforth.

Nairac entered the world in a small, huddling town in the north of England, a place where drizzling rain maintained a steady dance on the slate grey pavements, and people spoke in accents grown harsh and raw from the dampness. His father, Maurice, was a general practitioner while his mother, Barbara, attended to the welfare of her children and saw to the various tasks that fall to a busy doctor's wife. These were hectic times for Dr Nairac as he adjusted to the requirements of the National Health Service which was not yet one year old. One way and another, it seemed, everybody's world was in turmoil.

For Robert Nairac there were two worlds. First there was the flat-vowelled northern world into which he had been born, a place that was bounded by the cloth-capped realities of whippet racing, beer drinking and a male dominated working class culture that achieved its greatest fulfilment with a small win on the horses or a successful outing by the local football team. Beyond that lay the insulated world of culture, privilege and achievement to which money was the key. To enter by the door which Nairac used was expensive. It then cost almost twelve months of a working man's wage to pay for a year's board and tuition at his chosen school, Ampleforth.

For the 11-year-old Nairac admission to the school was the passport to a bright and golden future, but the glorious dream was marred three years later when his much-admired older brother, David, died suddenly and mysteriously at St Bartholomew's Hospital, London, where he had been a doctor. That left Nairac as the only surviving son. Family friends said that the hopes of his two older sisters were pinned heavily upon him.

The abbot of Ampleforth Abbey, to which the school was attached was Dom Basil Hume, later Cardinal Hume, the leader of Britain's five million Roman Catholics. Nairac left in 1966 with sufficient academic credits to ensure his entry to university. He had arrived at Gilling Castle, Ampleforth's preparatory school in 1960, transferring to the senior school two years later. By 17 he was head of St Edward's House and his name was on the honours board as a member of the rugby, cross-country and shooting teams. He was also school captain of boxing. He had made his mark both as a scholar and a sportsman, but there were those who believed he often retreated into a fantasy world in which he took on the role of some lone hero like Lawrence of Arabia.

Nairac fitted in naturally to an heroic mould, according to Mary Price who met him at an Oxford cocktail party. She recalled:

He immediately struck one as a very strong-minded person. He had a
cool, detached manner that was really different. I was swept off my
feet.

Nairac had been accepted as a university entrant to Sandhurst and
spent his vacations learning to be an officer. He was commissioned
into the Grenadier Guards six months before gaining his history
degree. During his time as a student he revived the boxing club at
the university and gained four Blues in matches with Cambridge as
well as playing in the rugby second XV. It was then that Mary
Price found herself moving into a romantic cul-de-sac.

Nairac, at Lincoln College on an army scholarship, had just
taken his finals, and she was in her first year at Ruskin School of
Art, before going on to teach handicapped children. Their back-
grounds were similar, the Catholic Church and membership of
England's minor squirearchy, based in the shires with their emp-
hasis on hunting, shooting and other field sports. To some extent
they belonged to an embattled class whose defensive paternalism
was under twin attack from the raging egalitarianism of the times
and the mocking incredulity of an age which saw its members as
futile anachronisms, clinging like limpets to old certainties that had
long since been exposed as hollow. Yet they hung on, maintaining
the silver links that binds the sons of Britain's landed interest to the
army and from there to the wider establishment.

One of Mary's brothers, like Nairac, went on to serve in a
Guards regiment. To the starry-eyed teenage girl, swept up in a
round of dinners and glittering military balls, Nairac looked like
the fulfilment of a dream. Their relationship blossomed and mat-
ured to the stage where they spent their weekends together, staying
with each other's parents and filling in the time with long country
walks or hunting with the falcon he kept and which was used in the
film 'Kes'.

He had a charisma about him. Funny thing was that he was very
gentle and very tough at the same time. I don't think he was quite as
serious about church-going as I was, but he had a strong religious
belief ... He was determined about what he wanted to do. He had to

39

do something out of the ordinary that was a challenge ...

Robert was enigmatic, but terribly charming. Over the years I could never quite work out whether my feeling for him was love or infatuation ... He was a tremendous romantic, but he had an element in him that, although he always seemed as if one day he intended to fall in love with a girl and settle down, first there was something very serious that he wanted to do.

I suppose I knew from the beginning that there was no real future for him and me because I knew how dedicated he was to the army. But I always hoped that he might come back from one army thing and everything would click into shape. But it was too much to expect ... Because his brother had died young I felt that he thought he must live up to a manly image.

She last saw Nairac at the glittering Chelsea Barracks Ball, one of the main social events of Britain's privileged classes, the year before he was killed. By that time he was heavily enmeshed in his undercover role in Ireland, and the signs were beginning to show. Somehow the carefree romantic had become buried beneath the skin of an older, graver man. Something had changed.

It was obvious his experience there had done something to him. He was very serious and very sober. His attitude was very much that what he was going to do was going to be difficult, so it was better not to be involved.

Mary, fair-haired and intense, delivered her own epitaph when she heard Nairac was dead.

Although I am very deeply upset, I feel that if he had to die he would have wanted to die in action.

BY THE EARLY 1970s the British army was well advanced in turning out a specialised type of warrior whose aggressive skills were honed by a process of brutalised primitivism. The aim was to produce an advanced killing machine, a self-propelled slayer robot who owed more to the Japanese Ninja assassin cults than to the mediaeval laws of chivalry whose lingering echoes continued to resound among European armies until recent times, even though they have received scant attention of late.

The type, grotesquely overdrawn, was depicted in the Rambo films made with chauvinistic abandon by the American actor Sylvester Stallone. Rambo was a caricature drawn from life. His real equivalents were to be found in the special forces being developed by most of the world's armies. For America this was the Green Berets and for Britain it was the Special Air Service. They were all looking for strong, capable men with a solitary streak and a taste for ruthless individual action. Nairac fitted neatly into the matrix.

There had been a post-war revision in military thinking, and some of the old distinctions that divided the permissible from the unthinkable had been eroded to the point where traditional notions of military gallantry had fallen away, to be replaced by the tough, pragmatic thuggery of a new and more realistic school whose members believed in a no-quarter approach to any perceived enemy.

That reality has been demonstrated in recent years by the French when their Paras, trying to hold down a popular uprising in Algeria, adopted an informal and unstated policy of shooting all village males who had reached puberty. They did this on the basis that if they did not shoot these beardless adolescents now they would probably have to shoot them next year when they might be armed.

The reality got another fillip in Vietnam when the Americans burned down villages and slaughtered their occupants, men, women and babies at the breast, to deny a haven to the Viet Cong. The same bloody reality was there on the streets of Derry on a bleak January day in 1972 when British paratroopers opened up on a crowd of unarmed demonstrators, murdering fourteen of them.

All of this caused some outrage among people who felt their own personal innocence was being ravished by such actions. There was less shock among the saddened people who had long since accepted the terrible truth which is that soldiers get paid to kill. It is more a matter of aesthetic than moral judgment to complain when they fail to cloak their task in shrouded decency, keeping it away from the eyes of the squeamishly polite.

The profession of arms has always been about converting unbelievers by slaughtering them in sufficient numbers to make the survivors amenable to reason. By the time Nairac became operational none of this had altered, but a changing world order had limited the available opportunities for the missionary mayhem of yesteryear.

The growling menaces of the USSR, China and the United States were held in a circle of taut antagonism which none dared to break for fear of terrible extinction. Britain, hanging on with bulldog determination to the remnants of her old prestige, aligned herself with the United States of America and deployed troops massively in the European front line of the Cold War.

This situation, which had persisted since the end of the Second World War, did little to satisfy the deep-seated and universal human urge for blood-letting, a sanguinary hunger which was somewhat alleviated by the hundreds of surrogate wars that raged continually in various parts of the world. It was against this background that a new military wisdom came to fruition. It taught that new challenges, as identified by the former Kenya campaigner, Major General Frank Kitson, were likely to arise from civilian insurrection as the discontented masses took to the streets in search of some sort of revolutionary purification.

To defeat these urban insurgents, the generals decided, it was necessary to train soldiers in such counter guerrilla techniques as infiltration, assassination, intelligence gathering and the various other areas of expertise that had been under continuous development since the days of the Second World War. Nairac became one of the beneficiaries of this new thinking. He was sent to Kenya to learn how to live off the land while functioning as a covert soldier, cut off from base and relying totally on his own resources.

During his field survival course he learned to breakfast on beetles and dine on raw rodents while concealing himself from the keen-eyed instructors who searched for him, blasting live rounds at any movement or other sign of his presence.

The training was the same as that undertaken by the Selous

42

Scouts, Rhodesian hard men named after an old African bush hand who roamed the land in the days when marauding tribesmen carried only knobkerries and assegais. That was at the turn of the century. Cecil Rhodes had just trekked north from the Cape, rolling up the country with a confident, acquisitive ease.

The Selous Scouts operated in a tougher terrain. Now the tribesmen carried Kalashnikov rifles and came roaring out of the bush to blast away with rocket propelled grenades and SAM 7s as they demanded their country back. Nobody was terribly surprised when they eventually got it.

Another trick Nairac learned was how to recycle his own urine to prevent dehydration. Most of the things he learned beneath that searing equatorial sun were like that: dirty, insanitary, smelly and repellent; enough to make a pig puke. Nairac may have gagged at some of the options that confronted him, but he took them. He was an urban sophisticate with a good degree, an Oxford accent and the unshakeable social assurance of his class. He was a superior being who was cheerfully allowing himself to be pushed back by the exigencies of the military life to the condition of a stone age man. He let it happen. Lawrence of Arabia could not have done it better.

Layer by layer the accretions of civilisation were stripped away from him, reducing him to a creature who responded with primitive directness to the stimulus provided by heat or cold, hunger or danger. At the level of reactive awareness Nairac had become a product of pre-history. He knew himself to be capable of subsisting at the instinctual level of animal survival, a rooting biped lurking in a neanderthal world of engulfing dangers.

He learned to move with a steady caution, ready at any time to substitute the instinctive ferocity of the snarling predator for the fugitive timidity of his secret, undercover role. Now he possessed all the attributes of a dangerous and powerful animal, ready to rend with mindless ferocity. It is not known how brightly the flame of manhood continued to burn within him. Nor is it known whether an animal attribute must always be purchased by the surrender of a corresponding human value.

Robert Louis Stevenson made literature out of the age-old conflict between good and evil, presenting it as the battle between

Dr Jekyll and Mr Hyde. Out in the sun-dried bush-lands the young officer carried out his own experiments in dualism, developing the Hyde factor, preparing to deploy all resources in the battle between light and dark.

After Kenya he flew back to Britain where as part of his continuing training he was posted to a secret establishment at Warminster where he learned the techniques of psychological warfare. Clearly by this time he had been bracketed as one of the new Ninja warriors, men selected for their toughness and intelligence. It would have been obvious to him from the direction his career was taking that he was on a fast track into military spheres where promotion and recognition arrived rather more quickly than it did for the traditional regimental officer.

From Warminster he joined the Special Air Service, having sought permission from his parent regiment, the Grenadier Guards. Officers on secondment to the SAS at that time served for about three years, which included their period of training. Captains normally stayed on at the Hereford base, serving as a troop commander with one of the unit's Sabre squadrons. Nairac was an exception. After he had mastered the covert techniques which enables the SAS to operate as silent killers behind enemy lines he moved on.

By 1974 he was in the north, first as a regimental officer leading a Guards platoon on patrol in Belfast and then as a member of an SAS detachment posing as 4 Field Survey Troop, Royal Engineers unit based in Castledillon, County Armagh. In case that was not enough to fool the curious the unit also operated under the covert name of the Northern Ireland Training and Tactics Team. This, NITAT, was the cover for recruiting murder gangs.

The country house in which the unit lived had once been a mental home. It was secluded and the undercover unit was guarded by Ministry of Defence police, a puzzling arrangement for active service soldiers who might have been expected to mount their own guards. The inevitable conclusion is that the people involved were too valuable to the army to have their time wasted on such routine military duties.

Suspicion grew among officers whose paths crossed that of the mysterious formation that what they were dealing with was a unit geared up for both intelligence gathering and secret kills. Major Fred Holroyd recalls that it came equipped with civilian Q cars, untraceable as army vehicles and fitted out with the most advanced communications equipment which was linked to a permanently manned operations room at Castledillon.

Members of the unit were issued with a range of weapons, some of them army standard issue, along with others which were recognised by soldiers as cowboy guns, the non-standard weapons issued to maverick units who had reason for not accounting for their activities.

Holroyd records:

> More ominously, in a cupboard in their armoury was a tray of 9mm Browning pistol barrels, extractors and firing pins which had been cast.

These were weapons which had been scrapped by the army having been declared too worn to be of further use. That is what the military means by 'cast'. The weapons were supposed to have been destroyed, and somewhere an officer's signature existed, attesting to the fact that he had witnessed their destruction. The discarded pistol parts served a useful purpose for those who wished to fire shots that could never be traced back to them.

A discarded barrel attached to an issue pistol would give an untraceable forensic reading and, since the weapon had been officially scrapped, the spare part could then be genuinely destroyed, blocking any possibility of a forensic trace. The same switch could be made with firing pins and cartridge extractors. This was standard procedure when the unit decided to take out a known republican and let the blame fall elsewhere. It was their way of muddying the statistics of death, and avoiding the embarrassing consequences of discovery.

Another layer of cover was added to the clandestine SAS unit with the addition of 14 Intelligence Company to its titles. These deceptions were necessary because British politicians kept denying that the SAS was in the north. The only ones who were not lying about this were the ones who had not been told. For the British government, anxious to assure the world that the Troubles amounted to no more than an eccentric outbreak of civil unrest involving a small group of politicised hooligans, the presence of the elite undercover formation was a grave, potential embarrassment. Was it really necessary to call in the British army's top killers to deal with an undisciplined and loutish rabble?

For a time Nairac led a Grenadier Guards platoon of foot soldiers who patrolled the hardline Shankill Road loyalist area of North Belfast. He was more interested in observing the nearby nationalist Ardoyne where someone had given the bemused Tommies the implausible task of holding down a civilian population grown mad with the bleak emptiness of scrap-heap living. A cold cruelty settled on the disputed streets as the arid struggle went on.

Those near to Nairac remember that he was appalled by the grinding level of poverty he saw around him. Worn women trailed their infant hostages into an uncertain future while middle-aged no-hopers slouched towards the sheltering haven of the bar-room. Young men, made dangerous by a steadily surging anger, strutted the streets with a challenging bravado, looking at the soldiers with cursing eyes. They were a generation born without hope, consigned at birth to a lifetime in limbo, under-educated and jobless. The ghost of poverty hung over them like a vapour.

Nairac saw all this, and he faced some grave questions of right and wrong amid the embattled fastnesses of Ardoyne, a place where bombs exploded nightly and bullets cut small lethal tunnels through the fabric of the days. They were questions which he ignored. He was surrounded by slaughterhouse images of gushing blood, shattered bones and lives gasped to an end on the hard, unyielding pavements. These were physical facts, lacking a moral dimension. It was sufficient for Nairac that he took a post in the real world where he could get on with what had to be done.

Maybe his schooling had something to do with that. Ampleforth, with an active cadet unit, has long had a reputation for producing army officers, particularly for the SAS whose founder, David Stirling, was educated there. Possibly because they are not directly involved in the military training programme the Benedictine monks of Ampleforth have been able to achieve at least one intellectually sophisticated feat. They have done this by apparently managing to reconcile the gentle pacifism of their divine master and the warlike activities of their cadet officer pupils.

As to the Catholics of Ardoyne and the wider fields of the north, any sympathy for their cause would have been either spurious or unthinkable since they were clearly British subjects who presumed to defy the authority of the crown. Nairac was a soldier who would carry out his duty.

Later, when Nairac was missing, and the British army and the Royal Ulster Constabulary were searching the South Armagh countryside for him, his 36-year-old sister Rosemond said at the walled family home at Stonehouse, Gloucestershire:

Since he has always loved Ireland and the Irish, it is ironic that he may have died while trying as a volunteer to contribute to peace in Ireland.

That may have been a comforting belief for the family, but for those on the receiving end of the army's peace-making efforts it raised an improbable image of a gentle, golden knight whose benevolence mantled the land beneath a comforting blanket.

The evidence says something different. It suggests that somehow time had slipped back a hundred years as Nairac strode across the Irish landscape, an avenging agent of the Imperial will whose soldierly skills were dedicated to thwarting the machinations of the scheming and sinister tribesmen who dared to defy the civilising mission of the Empire. For those who did not respond a sort of peace awaited. The peace of the grave.

There is also the blandishing thought that Captain Nairac loved the Irish. He may well have loved some of them; the saloon bar Irish, full of Paddy whackery and roguish Saturday night bullshit, the sort who carry a camouflaged personality for use as a defensive weapon, using it to create a sheltering fortification all around. The wandering soldier met more than his share of these as he toured the watering holes of South Armagh.

He certainly did not love the Irish who gave support to the

notion of a united Ireland, but maybe the visitations of death he wished upon them were tokens of a wider love for an Ireland he thought might be a better and happier place without their rebellious presence. Certainly its occupied portion would be more governable.

In the end Nairac was the product of his own fantasies, the central character in a dream world supported and shaped as much by his training and background as by the escapist heroics of his own imaginings. He took the key decision of his life on the dismal streets of Ardoyne when he put his moral judgment into cold storage and allowed the comfortingly neutral pressures of military duty to take over. With that action he laid the seeds of a tragedy which culminated with his painful and early death.

Before that happened it had probably made of him a murderer and the instigator of murder; certainly it turned him into a soiled conspirator, the controller of brutal and driven men whose killer lusts he harnessed to some immediate tactical purpose. He paid for that not only with his life but with the good name which a wearily opportunist government tried to redeem with the award of a medal for gallantry. They gave a George Cross to a pukka hero whose courage cannot be doubted, even as we weep for its flawed and misdirected abuse.

3

John Francis Green walked piously out of jail one mellow September day wearing the clerical suit that had been removed from his brother, the visiting priest.

A group of kidnappers had seized Father Gerry Green and stripped off his clothing to his underwear after which they bound and gagged him. Then they extended the priestly visit by locking Father Gerry in a broom cupboard and keeping him there until his Provo brother was far gone from the jail and filling his lungs with the sacred air of liberty.

Father Gerry, newly ordained, had gone to the Long Kesh detention camp to celebrate Sunday Mass for the 350 Catholic inmates who had been arrested and held without trial since the internment swoops of August 1971. Now one of them, John Francis, stepped out along freedom's road on a journey that was to end with his sudden and bloody death some two year's later.

For the embarrassed Long Kesh authorities this was the second escape of its kind. Eighteen months earlier, another internee, Francis McGuigan, had also walked out dressed as a priest.

John Francis Green, twenty-seven at the time of his escape from Long Kesh, was one of five brothers belonging to a staunchly nationalist family from Lurgan. He was high on the army's list when military units moved through the north in August 1971 to arrest suspected republicans.

He escaped then because he was not in the house when the soldiers smashed in the door and began their search. The word of the mass raids spread quickly around the Teaghnavan Estate and Green went on the run, hiding out in safe houses.

His luck ran out on 16 December 1971 when a military patrol spotted him on the Armagh–Portadown road, only miles from his home, and arrested him. He had stayed close to his roots, relying on a network of friends and supporters to warn him of impending dangers and offer him a place to hide. He was one of an army of uprooted men who scampered across the face of Ireland in an effort to avoid internment. Capture meant imprisonment without trial. So many fugitives poured over the border into County Louth that Dundalk, halfway between Belfast and Dublin, became known as Dodge City.

It quickly became clear that some of the arrest lists were out of date or based on defective information. Many of the interned men and women had long since ceased, for whatever reason, to be active members of the republican movement, but a good number of those captured were, in fact, republican activists. For these genuine hard men Long Kesh provided an opportunity to reinforce basic beliefs while perfecting the methods by which they might be turned into reality.

Classes in the Irish language ran side-by-side with demonstrations of bomb-making, while seminars on the techniques of urban guerrilla warfare merged into discussions of political theory. With hindsight the authorities were to dub Long Kesh a University of Terror. One of its graduates was John Francis Green.

As he made his way into the Republic, well ahead of the roadblocks and checkpoints that had been mounted following the belated discovery of his escape, he was more than equipped to take up his future role as a member of the senior command structure of the IRA. That made him just the sort of man that Captain Robert Nairac looked on as a prime target for assassination.

In his two years of liberty after fleeing Long Kesh, Green became one of the key participants in the wild and threatening game the IRA were putting on around the County Armagh area. He sought refuge in Castleblayney, just across the border in County Monaghan, but his IRA chiefs regarded him as too valuable to take off the active list. They needed someone who could both act as an enforcer and take command decisions. Green looked like the right man.

His first task was to tackle a problem of deteriorating discipline among IRA members in the hardline loyalist areas of Portadown and Lurgan. Internment had taken its toll in both towns and, in the absence of strong leadership, a hard drinking, womanising, group of fringe criminals had infiltrated the organisation, tearing its tightly disciplined structures apart and bringing it into disrepute.

Some of them were financing their social activities with unauthorised robberies while others were threatening shopkeepers and take-
away food outlets as they attempted to set up their personal extortion rackets.

To the men at the top, steeped in the mysticism of the blood
sacrifice, the one that was supposed to purchase freedom and dignity at the cost of a surrendered life, the treachery of these delin-
quents was unforgivable. Some of them were later found dead in
ignominious ditches, sent to a summary death by men who regarded their execution as no more significant than the cauterisation of a
stinking and septic pustule.

There were others who left the country, buying their safety at
the cost of banishment. Lesser offenders, such as drunks, were
merely expelled from the organisation, an exercise in clemency
which some of these ragtag rejects later repaid by turning low-
grade informer. Insurrections also create their own Augean stables.
Meantime the shadow of the Enforcer lengthened, stealing out
from its base in Monaghan to cover the entire county of Armagh.

The IRA, impressed by Green's efficiency, had given him
joint responsibility for Armagh county along with one of the area's
leading tacticians, Michael McVerry. They worked that way for a
very brief time for the hand of death was already reaching out for
McVerry. Much of their planning was done in the large, rambling
house which provided a safe haven in Castleblayney for men who
found themselves on the run. The partnership came to an end when
McVerry was shot dead during a raid on the joint military-police
barracks in the small republican stronghold of Keady on 15 Nov-
ember 1973. After that Green took operational control of the whole
county planning and organising attacks, which he sometimes led,
on the police and the army.

By the end of 1974 he was once again involved in an internal
enquiry into breaches of discipline within the IRA. Some of the
organisation's funds were missing and there was proof that some
unauthorised robberies had been carried out using IRA weapons.
Suspicion pointed at a man who was a close friend of Green. That
was a problem for Green. The Enforcer, filling his role as an IRA
leader, carried on with his investigation with dutiful determination

while Green the man lamented its punitive outcome.

As the year nudged towards its close there were faint glimmerings of hope that the five-year conflict might soon be diverted into more peaceful paths. A group of Protestant clergymen met leading members of the IRA in Feakle, a small settlement in County Clare, to try to thrash out a peace formula. They did this with the unofficial blessings of the British government which let it be known that there would be a more relaxed approach within the north at the time of the talks. The ceasefire was to last from 20 December until 2 January.

On the northern side of the border, and within Whitehall, there was a strong current of hostility towards the unofficially arranged ceasefire. It came from MI5 which suspected that the IRA had agreed to the cessation of hostilities to buy itself time while it regrouped and rearmed. The internal security service also suspected that it was being outflanked by its sister Secret Intelligence Service, otherwise known as MI6, which had played a large part in setting up the talks.

A fierce territorial war was then being waged between the two spook units for control of the intelligence operation in the north. The lines of demarcation were being erased as MI6, normally responsible for foreign intelligence, encroached on the territory of its domestic and disoriented rival. Observers at the time got brief glimpses of the political schizophrenia which triggered every irrational action of MI5, but few quite realised the extent to which its controlling pack of power-hungry reactionaries were prepared to go in support of their tainted, elitist and anti-democratic programme.

While members of MI5 nurtured their plans for a right-wing coup in Britain, aided by such senior former army officers as David Stirling, the founder of the SAS, they were ranged in the north against MI6. This was a rather more sophisticated organisation which was almost totally free of the constipated chauvinism of MI5, a condition to which the internal service was predisposed by its close links with the military.

The chiefs of MI6 believed that the longterm role of British intelligence in the north was to lay the groundwork for a political solution, even as they mounted a series of dirty tricks designed to keep the IRA off balance. In the meantime their relentless expansionism threatened to eradicate the rival MI5 as a force in the conflict. It was at this stage that the embattled chiefs of MI5 decided to discredit their rival by scuttling the continuing peace talks with an act of dramatic violence. Captain Nairac was their chosen instrument. John Francis Green was their target. They hoped his death would galvanise the IRA into a new outbreak of bombing and killing, ending the peace moves and restoring MI5 as the dominant intelligence service in the north.

Nairac's unit at Castledillon was under the direct control of MI5. It was responsible only to the internal security service for its actions, a procedure which left it completely free of the military chain of command. For some operations its members reported directly to a controller in London. Major Fred Holroyd, former military intelligence officer says in his book, *War Without Honour,* that during Nairac's undercover period MI5 drew the soldiers who handled civilian agents from both the Intelligence Corps and the SAS. He adds:

> Their policy was basic and shortsighted – use whatever means, legal or illegal, to blackmail the source into acting out of fear for his or her safety, then force them to carry out operations that cannot be traced back to the handler.

Analysis of Britain's intelligence war in the north points up the fact that low-grade informers and spies within the opposing communities were mainly run by non-commissioned officers. This was in accordance with techniques developed in such places as Kenya, Malaya, Cyprus and Aden. Counter gangs, trained to infiltrate enemy territory and assassinate named targets, were under the control of an officer. There have been four separate claims by members of loyalist killer gangs that their controlling officer was Captain Nairac.

They were not the only ones who came under his control. One of the men Captain Nairac was running was an established IRA member who had carried a gun for the republicans since 1971. He had been turned after being pulled in to Castlereagh Holding Centre for questioning and told to flee to Castleblayney, identified by the RUC as a republican nerve centre.

From this base he was to do great damage to the republican cause before running to the safety of a northern police barracks. He did that having fingered two members of the Irish National Liberation Army, Seamus Grew and Roddy Carroll, who were shot dead by police.

Before that happened the RUC plant was to pinpoint the whereabouts of Green, the Long Kesh escaper, for the three-man hit squad who were to cross the border to kill him. By that time the Christmas festivities had ended and the truce that held over the period of peace had run its hopeful, untroubled course. Then, suddenly, a maelstrom of madness once again swept across the fragmented deathscape and the new year, bloodied at birth, limped in to begin its scarred disintegration amid another volcanic firestorm of righteous hate.

The last mortal days of John Francis Green began with a furtive, night-time trip to his family home in Lurgan on Christmas Eve, 1974. He might have been arrested and thus saved from death, for the soldiers came knocking at the door while he was within the house. They stood there in camouflaged menace, asking questions and holding their guns at the port position, but they did not enter. The army had been told to suspend house searches for the duration of the ceasefire, so the squaddies made their call to let the Green family know they were being watched, and then they left.

The visit was enough to convince Green that he should be on his way back to Monaghan. He headed off on St Stephen's Day while there was still a week of the ceasefire to run, wearing a wig for disguise and wondering in amazement at the lack of checkpoints as his driver took him down the back roads that led down across the border to safety.

By early January he was deep into his investigation of the suspected theft of IRA funds, tied in with personal bank robberies carried out with the organisation's weapons. Those around him noticed that he was tense and abstracted. Later events were to show that the evidence he was gathering was equivalent to a death sentence for his friend. The IRA recovered that evidence, written up as a report and placed in an envelope, after he had been killed.

Shortly after 6 pm on 9 January 1975 Green left his safe house to drive his dark green Volkswagen up the heights to Gerry Carville's lonely farmhouse. The night was cold and wet and there was a wind whistling down off the Mullyash mountain, driving scuds of rain before it. The rain lanced down, dancing like small silver rods in the car's headlights. The road rose, glistening and black, crawling up the side of the rocky mountain like a slothful serpent.

Green was familiar with the two-storey farmhouse, for it was one of his regular places of refuge. Gerry Carville, the farmer, was a man with strong republican convictions and it amused many of the transient men who stayed there to know that they were under watch not only by the forces of the crown, but by the security forces of their own Irish Republic.

Since few of them had committed any unlawful act in the Republic they regarded the attentions of the garda special branch as being more than somewhat gratuitous. They became annoyed when British helicopters flew overhead. Gardaí raided the Carville farm in the autumn before Green was killed there, but they found nothing and there were no extradition facilities at that time for runaway IRA men who were regarded as political refugees.

On another occasion a platoon of British soldiers wandered across the border and searched Carville's house. Carville, returning from the rainy fields, found the soldiers sheltering in a hay-shed. The gardaí were alerted and raced along the highways and byways until they managed to discover the foot patrol. Then, with the enormous civility for which the Republic's police force is renowned, they ushered the straying soldiers gently back across the border to their own occupied part of the island, sparing them the tedious necessity of explaining their armed presence within the boundaries of the sovereign Irish state.

There was a lot of tension in the area around the time of the ceasefire, and immediately afterwards. Carville's house, marked down as a refuge for fleeing Provos, seemed to be getting a lot of attention from mysterious people. One night as he sat with a guest, Kevin Nugent, Carville heard a noise outside the house. Both went into the farmyard just in time to see two masked men running away towards a car that was parked up the lane. Some of the people around the mountain said they saw a white car, a Mercedes or an Audi, with three men in it. They appeared to be watching the Carville house. Garda investigations later confirmed the presence of the mystery car.

Carville remembers telling Green at the time: 'It's getting dangerous.'

Green nodded.

Most of the IRA men in the area took to sleeping with a gun at their side.

It was about 6.20 pm when Green arrived at Carville's house on that fateful night. The farmer had just finished a meal, but he offered to cook for Green. Green refused the food, but said he would take a cup of tea. Green was teetotal, and tea was his favourite beverage. The two men sat drinking their tea for some time and then Carville rose to go out. He helped out a neighbour every night by doing some milking.

He returned within the hour to a scene of disordered violence.

'When I landed at the front door, the door was lying wide, busted open,' he said. 'I looked in sideways and John Francis was lying on the flat of his back on the floor.'

Fearful and alarmed Carville ran to seek help. He found some neighbours, Joe Hamilton and Hugh William Clarke, walking on the road.

'I says: "Joe, John Green is dead".

'Joe says: "He's at his ould laughs again".

'Clarke says: "You'd better tell me, anyway".

'I says: "Willie, John Green's shot at the house".'

'He says: "Don't be talking".

'We went back. Me and Willie stayed out. I says to Joe Hamilton: "Joe, will you go over and look. Turn out the light for fear of somebody coming in".

'Joe came back and said: "He's shot, and well shot".'

THERE WERE THREE thousand people lining the streets as Green's remains were removed from Monaghan County Hospital to St Mary's Church three days after he had been gunned down. Relays of mourners carried the coffin through Monaghan town and a uniformed IRA guard of honour flanked the bearers as a lone drummer beat out the dead march. Ruairí Ó Bradaigh, President of Sinn Féin, told the sorrowing people that Green had been murdered, as moves were made to bring peace, by people who wanted to subvert that process.

Green, who left a wife and three children, was buried in his native Lurgan on 14 January. Members of the RUC saluted the cortege as it passed through the huge crowd which had assembled for the funeral. An IRA guard of honour waited near the church, unmolested by police who continued to act in the spirit of the fast-decaying truce.

The search was on for the killers. The RUC later came up with the theory that Green had been killed by a deranged Protestant called Elliott who believed the IRA had kidnapped his brother and taken him to Carville's farm where they had killed him.

The police theory was that Elliott brooded himself into madness and then went to Carville's house with an accomplice with the intention of killing the farmer. Carville was out, milking a neighbour's cows, when Elliott kicked down the door. Green hardly had time to realise what was happening when the avenging Elliott blasted the life out of him.

As a theory that is neat, plausible and flawed to the point of unbelievability. In the first place it was not produced until six years after Elliott's death and in the second no explanation was offered for how a deranged man found it so easily possible to find an accomplice for a murder mission. The accomplice claim would be more credible if it was also said that Elliott was a loyalist paramilitary, vengeful but sane, who called on a comrade for support.

No such claim was made, leaving us with the improbable suggestion that Elliott, deranged and out for blood, found it possible to recruit a helper who was untroubled by his lack of rationality. There was also the question of the weapons used. Forensic tests showed that Green had been shot by two guns, a Luger and a

Spanish made Star pistol.

A maddened countryman such as Elliott and his mysterious assistant, untainted by any suggestion of paramilitary or security force involvement, would have been unlikely to have had access to either weapon. They would have been more likely to have used shotguns. What is most interesting about this is that the RUC should have managed to identify a dead man as one of Green's killers while completely failing to discover the identity of his living accomplice.

This, of course, is the most complete nonsense. The fact is that the late Mr Elliott, sane or otherwise, has had his reputation besmirched to provide a scapegoat for the Green killing, thereby shielding the real killers from public exposure. His mysterious accomplice, who should have been traceable since Elliott was a man with limited social contacts, was dragged in to provide an explanation for the second weapon.

No attempt appears to have been made to link Elliott and the other man to the white car seen around Carville's farm. That in itself is decidedly suspicious, since it would have been a matter of mere routine to discover whether the accused man or any of his acquaintances had a car which fitted the description. Nor was any effort made to link Elliott and his alleged accomplice to the two masked figures seen fleeing from Carville's yard.

The fact that none of this was done may be charitably described as a piece of crass ineptitude. More realistically it might be called an exercise in the sort of overweening arrogance that believes claims from establishment sources never need to be substantiated.

A lot of the evidence is in now on the Green murder, and while there is no absolute proof that Captain Nairac was ever in Carville's farmhouse pumping bullets into the unfortunate Green, the mass of circumstantial detail, together with the claims of Major Holroyd, makes it difficult to resist the belief that the SAS officer played a prime role in the murder.

Fred Holroyd says that a smiling Robert Nairac stood in his office one January day in 1975 and said that he had killed John Francis Green, one of the top Provos operating in the border area.

When Holroyd looked at him in amazed disbelief Nairac produced a Polaroid picture of Green lying dead in his own blood in the flagged parlour of Gerry Carville's farmhouse. Holroyd says that there was a square of darkness on the wall where an uncurtained window held out the bleak, winter night.

It was through that window, Nairac told him, that he and another man had watched Green before kicking in the door and emptying their guns into his reeling body. They had known where he was hiding, Nairac said, and three of them had driven across the border to get him.

'He told me he had killed Green, together with two other men who I assumed were Staff Sergeant B and the Sergeant Major as they worked as a team,' Holroyd recalls. 'They had crossed the border without interference and driven down the country road to Gerry Carville's farm. They knew Carville would leave at a specific time. This he did.'

Holroyd took the photograph out of Nairac's hand and asked if he could keep it. He was building up souvenirs of the north, making a record of all the interesting things that happened during his tour of duty. Nairac, he recalls, was not too happy about parting with the photograph, but he gave it up anyway. Holroyd thinks that Nairac wanted his job and, more particularly, his contacts when he left the north, so he handed over the picture to keep relationships sweet. Later, when the RUC were investigating the army's use of dirty tricks Holroyd says he gave the picture to a superintendent to help with his enquiries.

He never did get it back and repeated requests for its return have been met with the claim that it is in the interests of state security for the police to keep it. That is a puzzling story whose mystery increased when a picture, purporting to be the one Nairac gave to Holroyd, was first offered to the *Sunday Times* in London and rejected as a phony and then published in the more trusting *Independent*.

After Holroyd made his claim that Nairac was one of Green's killers it was suggested that Nairac, acting the role of a glory boy fantasist, had invented his part in the Green murder. That is just one of the official claims that fails to make sense. If Nairac did that then it can only have been to impress Holroyd, a supposition that suggests such a level of immaturity as to make one wonder how he ever got through the officer selection tests. It is possible, of course, since maturity has never been one of the prerequisites of a successful soldier, but it still leaves unanswered the question of why Nairac should lie to impress Holroyd.

The more reasonable explanation is that he was neither lying nor out to impress. He was merely telling a colleague, whose line of work in military intelligence was close to his own, about a successful operation in which he had been involved, a matter of professional interest to both men. There are few trades in which the participants do not talk shop.

To the claim that Nairac may have lied Holroyd comments:

> I can only relate that Robert Nairac said quite plainly that he had been involved in the killing ... I had no reason to disbelieve what Nairac told me, any more than the Protestant terrorists who have since admitted that they met him and liaised with him over such activities. What made me certain that he knew what he was talking about was that when the evidence emerged from the garda enquiry it tallied closely with Nairac's account.

This evidence showed that the door had been kicked in causing precisely the damage to the frame which Nairac had spoken about before the facts became public. It confirmed Nairac's statement that the death room had been uncurtained. There was also Nairac's claim that two guns had been fired at Green. Tests showed that this was indeed so. There is also the fact that Nairac had the Polaroid death picture. The possession of that picture suggests that he possessed a damning degree of guilty knowledge of the killing, since he would have been unlikely to have had the picture without this.

What does need looking at is Holroyd's claim that Nairac told him that, along with two others, he killed Green. Holroyd assumed the two others were the two senior non-commissioned officers who made up Nairac's team. Later events were to show that Nairac did not always work with these soldiers.

There is a mystery about why Nairac failed to name his two

60

accomplices. He was talking to a brother officer, a man with a professional interest. The suspicion inevitably arises that Nairac did not put names to his accomplices because that would have exposed the fact that he was working with a murder gang rather than with his irregular military unit.

There are other apparent contradictions. Martin Dillon writes that Green was killed by two Portadown loyalist paramilitaries, one of whom was later involved in planning the Miami Showband Massacre. That theory, now widely held by investigators, followed the earlier smokescreen, claims that Green was the victim of a solitary loyalist gunman.

This lone gunman suggestion is a piece of insulting nonsense which relies on the existence of a two-handed gunman, blazing away at Green with a Luger in one hand and a Star pistol in the other, performing the sort of feat that has rarely been seen since the days of Wild Bill Hickock. The alternative explanation is that the gunman shot Green first with one pistol and then with the other. Given that sort of lethal determination it is a wonder he did not also hang, stab, poison and defenestrate the unfortunate corpse to ensure it was suitably and permanently dead. There is no need for this unmitigated rubbish to detain us any further.

What does merit closer examination is the separate evidence tying the shadowy figure who Dillon calls 'Mr A' – a man still powerfully present among the north's loyalist paramilitary gangs – into the Green killing. This man, more usually known as The Jackal, was in fact the major planner behind the Miami killings, but none of the men who could convict him will talk in a courtroom. Others who might are dead, one of them by natural causes.

The Jackal forms the vital link between Nairac, the Green killing and the Showband massacre. It is now possible to say that one of the men who murdered Green was a young UVF member, Harris Boyle, later to become a major in the organisation. He died while planting a bomb in the Miami bus. The Jackal was his loyalist controller on the Green killing. He was also the third man at Mullyash.

For Captain Nairac the relationship with The Jackal was both efficient and rewarding. As a leading loyalist activist, blooded and unafraid, The Jackal had connections with both the UDA and the UVF. He combined this with the ability to put together at short notice armed units whose members might be drawn from either organisation. In other cases he was able to reinforce his gangs with members of the 10,000 strong Ulster Defence Regiment, armed and paid for by the British government.

He was, and is, a man of rather more intelligence and substance than the average tattooed and swaggering loyalist gunman. As such he was Nairac's primary link into the murky world of the Protestant hard men. He was the fixer who provided the loyalist gunmen for Nairac to use against the IRA. At least four of these gunmen have identified Nairac as the man who gave them their briefings. Not all of those who knew about Nairac's role lived to talk about it.

One of these, a 28-year-old Protestant disc jockey, was killed by the IRA because of his association with Harris Boyle. What his killers did not know was that he was one of Nairac's main informants. They got the name Norman 'Mooch' Kerr when they stole a diary from Boyle's clothing while he was swimming in Portadown public baths.

Kerr, who had been introduced to Nairac by Boyle, owned a mobile discotheque which he took to bars in the mainly Protestant town of Banbridge on four nights a week. On one or two other nights he played in public houses in Armagh, moving freely into nationalist bars where strangers were viewed with suspicion and sometimes taken out for questioning. That never happened to him. His job as a disc jockey provided perfect cover for his information gathering operations.

His brief was merely to keep his ears open and report back anything that might be of interest. Additionally he would be shown albums of photographs and asked to watch for the people pictured so that he could tell Nairac about their movements, who they were associating with and whether they appeared to be involved in any unusual activity.

He worked for a long time around the Catholic bars of Armagh city, an unmolested small town celebrity living on the fringes of the entertainment industry. Then the IRA found his name in Harris Boyle's diary. That was guilt by association and the penalty was death.

Three of them, armed and wearing masks, arrived at the Carrick Bar in Market Street, Armagh city shortly after midnight on 14 August 1975 while 'Mooch' Kerr was packing up his disco gear. Two of them posted guard on the door and the third man, a tall, lithe young fellow with a swinging stride, went up behind Kerr and shot him in the nape of the neck with a careless professionalism.

If Nairac had thought about Kerr's murder he might have made the connection between death and deceit, might even have contemplated the dangers that lurked within the apparently welcoming walls of a public house. He did neither of these things because he had other preoccupations. Spies were expendable. The Jackal would find a replacement.

The Jackal's contacts made him a valuable ally of the young SAS officer whose shadowy role begins to take on a rather more guiltily solid shape with the appearance of such sinister cohorts. Fellow officers now say that Nairac's methods of operations make it almost certain that he was running pseudo-gangs involved in both killing and intelligence gathering.

A former member of Britain's Intelligence Corps said:

Nairac was quite obviously involved in taking out key IRA players and to do this he was using loyalist gangs, helping them to carry out the killings. From a military point of view what he was doing was both unexceptionable and intelligent.

He was using native manpower to carry out catch-and-kill operations in which neither he nor the army had any apparent involvement. This was an exemplary application of the techniques refined during the colonial insurrections – a textbook example of how to control and operate a pseudo-gang of the sort developed by General Kitson in Kenya. Add to that the SAS tactic of getting behind enemy lines to assassinate enemy leaders and it is clear that he was running a brilliant little operation. The only surprising thing is that the opposition allowed him to go about his business so openly.

4

By the middle of the twentieth century the subject tribes of Africa were beginning to shake off the torpid fatalism with which they had accepted their imperial serfdom. The wheel of history was turning, exposing a dithering indecision where once there had been prideful assurance. Suddenly the colonised peoples were sensing a growing debility among those who presumed to rule over them. Uncertain economic and social conditions, along with a weakening resolve among the European overlords, combined to lay the foundations for a white withdrawal.

The palmy days were over and it was nearly time to go. A libertarian contagion was spreading throughout the world and it was becoming increasingly clear that, for better or worse, the day of the imperial dynasty was done. This was a development that was greeted with a listless apathy by the mass of Britons who had never truly benefited from their country's imperial possessions.

At the height of empire, as Britain's possessing classes grew butter-fat on the expropriated wealth of other nations, there were more than 100,000 forlorn women offering their bodies on the streets of London for the few pitiful pence needed to buy a meal or a bed for the night. It is unlikely that they were all there as the result of invincible wickedness, despite the strictures of Victorian moralists. Quite simply they were the unfortunate victims of a grossly hypocritical society whose moralistic posturings they could not afford to share.

The empire needed a huge standing army and, for the transposed slum-dwellers and country boys who served in the ranks, marriage was often impossible since they were not paid enough to support a wife and family. One consequence of this was that one in five of Queen Victoria's soldiers suffered from venereal disease. Their pauperised brothers and sisters lived out malnourished lives in the shadow of the workhouse, escaping from the fetid realities of a demeaning cockroach poverty into an easeful state of gin-sodden amnesia. Whatever benefits the empire might have conferred upon

Britain were clearly not distributed evenly throughout the nation.

Exploitation, like charity, began at home, and it is one of the mocking ironies of history that those who provided the muscle and the manpower which enabled their social superiors to set up an imperial conspiracy for the systematised looting of much of the planet, should themselves be among its first victims.

It is not surprising there were few of this class who mourned the passing of empire, but there were some sad remnants of its blown and faded grandeur who turned away from the comfortless path of progress. These were the left-over people who sought shelter in a twilight nostalgia even as they comforted themselves with a forlorn belief in the power of their wasting sword arms. That particular delusion was widespread. In the disordered decades that followed the fading of imperial powers, Britain, France, Holland, Belgium and even the interventionist USSR and United States of America, paid the price of this martial delusion, seeding the earth of hostile lands with their sacrificed dead.

For an embattled post-war Britain, honour, self-respect and the need to reaffirm old beliefs became increasingly engaged as the empire lay convulsed in its agonising death throes. Much of that agony was borne by other people. India, the jewel in the imperial crown, was abandoned in such inglorious haste that two million people died in the civil war that erupted in the power vacuum which Britain left behind.

A year later, in 1948, there was another post-imperial trauma as Britain scuttled out of Palestine, fleeing the sophisticated terrorism of an increasingly confident Jewish guerrilla army. The Palestinians paid the price for that unseemly abdication. Many of them died and a million men, women and children were forced to flee, creating the massive refugee problem which continues to bedevil Middle East politics. If these situations were not so demonstrably the result of a panic-stricken and monumental incompetence it might easily be thought that they had been brought about by a malicious will to exact a parting penalty.

Britain's resolve to hold on stiffened when the title to its pleasantly luxurious equatorial possession in Kenya came under attack from a tribe of badly-armed and largely untrained insurgents, mostly underfed and tattered as scarecrows. These were the Mau Mau. What they lacked in arms and training they more than made up for in fanaticism.

Members of the Mau Mau were recruited almost exclusively from the Kikuyu tribe and they were bound together by fearful oaths taken in forest clearings. During the oath-taking ceremony they masturbated over a dead fish, smeared themselves with menstrual blood and drank from a bowl that had been filled with the blood of all the oath takers whose arms were slashed for the purpose. Although many of them were later turned, working enthusiastically for the British against their former comrades, the power of the oath was sufficient to ensure the loyalty of most Mau Mau members.

Almost all of their violence was turned against Kenyan blacks who served the colonial settlers, mostly as house servants or farm workers. Women were raped and otherwise outraged while men were mutilated and killed with pitiless cruelty. Farm stock provided a favoured target and the Mau Mau specialised in a type of agrarian economic warfare against the white settlers.

They maimed cattle, destroyed crops, burned down farm buildings and spread such fear among the rural blacks that the land quaked in terror at close of day. Only about two dozen whites died at the hands of the Mau Mau whose campaign flared most fiercely in the four years from 1952. It lessened when, in 1956, the British government began to treat with Kenyan political leaders. Seven years later, on 12 December 1963, the country was granted full independence.

The Mau Mau rising was into its first year when a young subaltern was summoned from the Mess of the first battalion of the Rifle Brigade, then stationed in Germany, to be told he was being posted to special duties in Kenya. Frank Kitson, later to become a major general and the British army's leading expert on irregular warfare, was to spend the next two years in a small camp in the African bush refining the techniques of counter-insurgency.

Kitson arrived in Kenya in the middle of 1953 to find a scene of political and military confusion. The Mau Mau were ranging freely across the 240,000 square miles of Kenyan territory, a ragged network of savage avengers who melted easily into the surrounding tribal structures as they went about their desperate and savage work. Local intelligence was so scarce that it was thought all Mau Mau actions were guided by one supreme commander, believed to be Jomo Kenyatta who was to become Kenya's first president after a protracted spell in jail. The gangs were in fact run by a central committee composed of one representative from each of the Kikuyu native reserves.

The militarised police force was at full stretch in trying to contain the stealthily vicious challenge to British rule. Kitson, who was to be awarded a Military Cross and be promoted to major for his two year's work in Kenya, was attached to the police special branch. He was moved up-country with some other Europeans and a nucleus of Africans, all of them charged with the task of destroying the Mau Mau.

The black collaborators were given the spearhead role and sent out to find the terror gangs and the villages which supported them. They were told to take the horrific oath. Some of them took part in Mau Mau raids, maiming beasts and torturing farm servants, as a way of establishing themselves as committed terrorists.

Within weeks the names of disaffected villages started to feed back to the British authorities. Police and military mounted a series of mass arrests as villages were stripped of their male populations. The interned Kikuyu were set to work building two camps to house themselves. Mau Mau prisoners who had been turned were hooded and shown the lines of arrested men, peering at them through cut-out eye-holes.

Hidden informers pointed out their former comrades to eager policemen who then took them away for the sort of punishing interrogation in-depth that is only ever acknowledged by the bruised bodies and broken bones of its victims. Slowly the innocent were separated from the guilty and returned to their homes. Some of those who remained opted to work for the British. They were moved to the up-country camp for special training as part of a military reaction force.

Kikuyu were sent out dressed in ragged coats and patched trousers. Mostly they went barefoot, but occasionally one of the gang would wear a pair of down-at-heel shoes, scuffed and broken. They all wore strings of beads around their necks. Battered trilby hats were much in demand. Their dress was typical of a Mau Mau terrorist. To add a further note of realism, they also carried the same sort of home made guns as the Mau Mau, only theirs were more lethally effective.

When a village was terrorised by a gang, the headman chopped to pieces, babies bludgeoned to death and the women raped, there was really no way of knowing whether the perpetrators were genuine Mau Mau or opportunist collaborators seizing the chance to create some freelance mayhem. Once the pseudo-gang was out in the bush they controlled their own operations. They could behave as viciously as they wished, knowing that blame for their worst actions could always be shifted on to the real Mau Mau.

The attack against the insurgents was two-pronged. Joint military and police patrols engaged the terrorists in the field. Kitson reports a typical series of incidents:

> In the evening, after General Erskine's visit, Jacky Miller took out a military patrol and captured a gang leader with ten of his gang. Miller and a police patrol killed four terrorists and captured another out of a gang of nine. Two days later he killed five more.

While this was happening plans were being made to round up some 100,000 men in Nairobi. The intention was to identify the 70,000 Kikuyu estimated to be among them so that they could be sent to detention camps. A hard core of 10,000 Mau Mau activists was expected to be held after screening. Families of the arrested men were to be sent to the Kikuyu native reserves. There was, of course, no suggestion that any of these people would face a court of law.

Legions of men were locked up, but inexplicably their detention did not halt the insurrection, any more than the concentration camps, invented by British generals to hold Boer guerrilla fighters and their families, brought an end to the South African war of 1899–1901. When internment was tried again in the north in the early 1970s with hundreds of republicans being plucked from their beds it failed there too.

In some ways Britain's campaign against the Mau Mau provided a blueprint for its later battle against the IRA. In a move that prefigured the accommodation arrangements at Long Kesh prison, set amid the quiet greenery of County Down, Mau Mau suspects arrested during the great Nairobi round-up, were held in cages. There are also certain similarities in the techniques used for turning insurgents in both Kenya and the north. Kitson recounts that when a suspect was first held he would be treated harshly with the object of diminishing any idea he might have of himself as some sort of hero.

That was a pattern followed in the north where attempts were made to break prisoners by means condemned as inhuman and degrading by the European Court of Human Rights. As in Kenya determined efforts would be made to turn the more amenable prisoners into military informers or police agents. There were necessary differences in approach since the security forces operating in the north carried out their campaign in largely urban areas in which suspects were in daily contact with friends and families.

In Kenya the target terrorists were shipped away to the bush camp where they first had to win the approval of the other Kikuyu before being gradually accepted. They were then treated in a friendly way, but not told too much until they were considered ready for the next step along the road to full commitment. This came with an indication from the Mau Mau member that he wished to be fully absorbed into the community of betrayal. From then on everything was open to him. He was allowed to sleep and train with the other defectors, carry arms and stand solo sentry duty. All the indications were that he was now a trusted member of the group. The psychological pressures to conform to the group will were inexorable.

There was no way that the military or police could duplicate this operation in the north, but there was the continuing need to provide some semblance of a secure environment for the turned terrorist. Occasionally a captured paramilitary with a lot of background information would be taken off to a remote and comfortable hotel for a lengthy debriefing by his handler, but that was far from being a routine operation. An alternative support structure was laid down.

This relied on the intelligence controller, whether police or military, developing a close, friendly and paternalistic relationship with his agent who would then come to be almost totally reliant on him for everything from beer money to approval. It was a system that frequently failed to work, and the hedgerows of Ireland stood sentinel over many a lifeless piece of evidence to its failure. When failure did happen it was more frequently the fault of the agent, nervous and mostly self-absorbed, than his controller. This was a person who had been taught to live by the protective lie, a masterful illusionist who moved between dissimulation and manipulation with poised assurance.

General Kitson has this to say on the subject:

> Intelligence officers find themselves developing a new set of characteristics such as deviousness, patience and a determination to outwit their opponent by all means compatible with the achievement of the aim. Those who are not capable of developing these characteristics are inclined to retreat into their military shells and try not to notice what is going on.

There is more than a clue there to the sort of character developed by Captain Robert Nairac. The general's observations also give a strong indication of how other military officers managed to remain in almost total ignorance of what Nairac was doing.

ONE QUALITY WHICH Kitson neglects to mention in setting out the make-up of an intelligence officer is the raw, naked courage that is often needed. The annals of British military history are full of spontaneous acts of outstanding gallantry, but they also contain many examples of the sort of sustained bravery that is ultimately more admirable than the quicksilver moment of transient heroism. There is also the lesson that those who pursued the imperial dream often did so to the point of a fatal but dutiful self-sacrifice.

Sometimes, as with Captain Colin Mackenzie, their sacrifices stopped short of death. Before retiring as a lieutenant-general he took more than 24 enemy bullet and knife wounds. It is a tradition of which every young British officer is made fully aware. For Nairac, a man in search of a manly role, the pages of history provided both a source of inspiration and role models aplenty.

In 1832 Alexander Burnes, a 27-year-old officer in the service of the British East India Company, obtained permission to lead an expedition into Central Asia with the aim of securing trade treaties with local rulers. The young officer, a distant relation of the Scottish rhymester, Robert Burns, led his party over the sheer face of the Hindu Kush across Afghanistan and north of the Oxus river to the violent emirate of Bokhara. There they were first threatened with death by the xenophobic ruler, the Emir Nasrullah, and then made to wear black capes and ropes around their necks. The cape was the mark of the foreign invader; the rope was a tangible reminder of the fact that all men lived in servitude to the benevolent Nasrullah.

The visiting party, which endured many dangers and hardships, were also threatened with a deep well full of cockroaches, snakes and other crawling horrors that lived off the rotting corpses of those who had displeased the ruler. Living prisoners were chained around the edge of the well, waiting to be thrown in. During his trip Burnes met the Afghan ruler, Dost Mohammed, a man who was later to prove extremely troublesome to the expansionist British. Back home to a hero's welcome the feted soldier was hailed as Bokhara Burnes.

He was more fortunate than two other officers who were to follow him to Bokhara, which lay just east of the Persian border with Afghanistan. Colonel Charles Stoddart went into the savage emirate, which lies athwart the old Mongol route to the west, to try to forge an alliance against the Russians who were beginning to menace Britain's eastern empire. Stoddart was seized and thrown into a stinking pit hollowed out of the mud beneath the palace square. When he did not return Captain Arthur Connolly was sent to look for him. He too was plunged into the rat-ridden hole.

Some months later both men were brought out into the blazing sunshine on a midsummer morning in 1842. They were half-starved and covered with sores and rat bites. Lice moved freely in their hair and beards, trailing a verminous network across the soldiers' gaunt frames. The prisoners knelt with their arms tied tightly behind their backs until the executioner came and took off Stoddart's head with a strong, efficient swipe, closely followed by Connolly's.

It was a further reminder that, while there was fame, honour and glory to be won, those who sought such baubles had to be stoically prepared to pay the darker price of imperial voyaging. They lived in a world of cold cruelties peopled by unfeeling despots who placed no value on human life. It was a world in which practical men dictated that self-interest must always take precedence over either compassion or toleration. The barbarities of eastern rulers shocked the people of Britain even as they watched their fellows being hanged for stealing sheep.

The times were boisterous, red-blooded and impatient of subtlety. They called for ready-made heroes and Lieutenant Eldred Pottinger fitted the role to perfection. Pottinger was a member of that incredible breed of junior British officer who glided from one outpost of empire to another, disguised in native dress and prattling away fluently in the local dialect while gathering information and forging alliances that were to shape the destiny of nations.

On an August day in 1837 Pottinger, 26 years old, found himself in Herat, an Afghan city coveted by Persia. His skin was dyed a light walnut brown and he was posing as a Muslim holy man. He was in Herat for two reasons. Britain, which had designs on Afghanistan, needed first hand intelligence of the city's defences, and there was also need to assess its vulnerability to attack by either the Russians from the north or the Persians from the west. Pottinger was in Herat for only a bare few days when Persia attacked.

Pottinger, mindful of his duty to preserve the city for possible future incorporation into the British empire, immediately offered his services to Yar Mohammed, the vizier who was directing the defence. The siege lasted for ten months, producing the usual sickening scenes of starving people catching and eating rats. Pottinger's biographer, Sir John Kaye, wrote:

His activity was unfailing. He was always on the ramparts; always ready to assist with his counselling, and to inspire with his animating presence new heart into the Afghan soldiery.

The siege ended with a Persian withdrawal after Britain sent a naval squadron to threaten the attackers western region in the Persian Gulf.

A soldier of an equally positive, if rather more stern and punitive disposition, was Captain John Nicholson. In 1852 he was dispatched to the lawless Bannu district, south-west of Peshawar on India's rebellious north-west frontier. His instructions were to pacify the troublesome natives, described as 'the most savage and ignorant of all frontier Pathans'. British authority languished as the fierce hillmen went busily about their traditionally pleasurable pursuits of murder, robbery, rape and pillage.

In Nicholson they had been sent a law-giver of harsh and unyielding temperament. This had been demonstrated very clearly by his suggestions for punishment following the Indian mutiny. The troops had risen when Muslim soldiers were given cartridges greased with pig fat. Their religion taught that contact with any part of a pig would condemn them to hell. After the mutiny Nicholson was severely critical of what he regarded as the merciful practice of blowing convicted native soldiers from the mouths of cannon. Such a death was too quick for them, he said.

He suggested instead that they should be given more time to contemplate their misdeeds as they were flayed alive, burned over a slow fire or impaled on bamboo stakes. It took Captain Nicholson just three months to bring the disorderly Pathans to heel.

The tree from which Nicholson hanged offending Pathans still stands in Bannu today. There is only one branch left, but it is still heavily scored with the rope marks made by men who kicked their way into eternity with their heads in a vengeful noose. The lightest punishment doled out by Nicholson was to order an offender to be flogged senseless. There was a human skull on his desk, a grim memento which Nicholson used to impress visitors. It belonged, he said, to a savage dacoit, a murderous robber. Nicholson had chopped the head off with one stroke of his cavalry sabre.

73

He was very conscious of his dignity as a representative of the empire. One unfortunate visiting chief had his beard forcibly shaved off for neglecting to bow to Nicholson. When the enraged man spat on the floor in protest he was made to lick it up. Nicholson, who clearly preferred soldiering to administration, was a man of few words. One of his reports read: 'I have the honour to inform you that I have just shot a man who came to kill me.'

The tradition of the British army spy was well advanced by the time Francis Younghusband was born on a hill station at Muree, on the north-west frontier. He subsequently joined the 1st King's Dragoon Guards where he served as a lieutenant before being moved to intelligence work. In 1877 he was in Manchuria, posing as a native trader, probing Chinese defences when he bumped into his heavily disguised colonel, Mark Bell, who was there on a similar mission. After a discussion about how they might avoid duplication of effort Younghusband, aged 24, was told to take the high road back to India to see if he could discover a new route.

He left Peking in the spring at the start of a wearing and hazardous journey that was to last seven months as he battled against first the baking heat of the desert and then the bone-chilling cold of the mountains. He arrived in India after scrambling across the roof of the world, which he tackled without either climbing or high altitude equipment, coming down off the snowbound Karakorams where they meet the heart-stopping Hindu Kush, Pamir and Himalaya ranges in rocky and forbidding grandeur. For that journey he was honoured by being made the youngest member of the Royal Geographical Society.

Two years later he embarked upon an even greater adventure. He had been planning to go to the forbidden city of Lhasa, made up as a Yarkandi trader, when he was detailed to find a secret pass through the Pamir mountain chain which caravan raiders were using as an escape route having staged one of their sorties. The British authorities suspected that Safdar Ali, the ruler of Hunza, was behind the caravan raids so Younghusband was also given the task of telling the mountain ruler to desist. He set out to do both these errands with an escort of six Gurkha soldiers.

After a steep climb up the mountains to the village of Shahidula there was news of the mysterious Shimsal Pass. It was set high on a sheer cliff and dominated by a fortress occupied by the caravan raiders. A river ran through the gorge which lay below it. Younghusband posted four Gurkhas to give cover, crossed the frozen river with his two NCOs and scrambled up the precipitous cliff face. As they approached the fort, the gates which had been opened, were suddenly slammed shut. Years later Younghusband remembered:

> In a flat second the whole wall was lined with the wildest looking men, shouting loudly and pointing their matchlocks at us from fifty feet above.

These villainous-looking men not only plundered caravans, they murdered their guards and sold young, strong or comely captives into slavery. As the soldiers stood, waiting for the raiders to fire, two men came out to invite them into the fort, but when Younghusband raised the imperial objections to caravan raiding with the leaders they said they could not discuss this. Next day the British party set off with an escort of seven Hunzas to see Safdar Ali in his mountain fastness.

Safdar Ali had something in common with Captain Nicholson, the owner of the severed head. He was also a man of strong and positive action. He assumed the throne of Hunza after personally slaughtering his mother and father and hurling his two brothers over a precipice. Ali, who believed that Younghusband was an emissary from some petty tribal chief anxious to seek his favour, kept him standing. The irritated officer sent one of his soldiers for his camp stool and set it alongside the surprised ruler's throne. To reinforce the message he told the Gurkhas to fire off a few rounds to demonstrate the superiority of their firearms over the muzzle-loading matchlocks of the Hunza tribesmen. An impressed Ali then asked the Gurkhas to demonstrate the accuracy of their weapons by shooting some of his subjects off the opposite cliff.

Back at base a disgusted Younghusband confirmed British suspicions that Safdar Ali was plotting with the Russians, and that the scoundrelly fellow was unrepentantly committed to continuing his attacks against caravans, even those carrying British goods. He recommended military action against the treacherous ruler, commenting:

> I knew that he was a cur at heart and unworthy of ruling so fine a race as the people of Hunza.

The Earl of Pembroke, also known as Strongbow, was another cur unworthy of ruling anybody. He landed in Ireland in 1169 and proceeded to set the houses of the dissident natives on fire having nailed their owners to the door by their ears.

By the time of the Tudor dynasty Queen Elizabeth was uttering such thoughts as: 'We must raise an army for the protection of the realm and the suppression of the Irish'. Centuries later the government of her royal namesake were still dispatching capable chaps like Nairac for much the same purpose.

William Lecky, the English historian, said of one of the Virgin Queen's campaigns:

> The war, as conducted by Carew, by Gilbert, by Pelham, by Mountjoy, was literally a war of extermination. The slaughter of Irishmen was looked upon as literally the slaughter of wild beasts. Not only the men, but even the women and children who fell into the hands of the English were deliberately and systematically butchered. No quarter was given to prisoners who surrendered, and the whole population was skilfully and steadily starved to death.

Another contemporary witness, Edmund Spenser, the poet who had been given a 4,000 acre estate in Cork for his services to the crown, wrote a book, *View of the Present State of Ireland*. He says of the survivors of that campaign:

> Out of every corner of the woods and glens they came creeping forth upon their hands, for their legs could not bear them. They looked like anatomies of death; they spoke like ghosts crying out of their graves. They did eat the dead carrion, happy when they could find them. Yea, and one another soon after, in as much as the very carcasses they spared not to scrape out of their graves.

76

In the province of Ulster the army led by Mountjoy, a man whose name was to be commemorated in the name of Dublin's jail, established his supremacy with a campaign of merciless butchery. A witness reported:

> No spectacle was more frequent in the ditches of towns, and especially in wasted countries, than to see multitudes of these poor people dead, with their mouths all coloured green by eating nettles, docks, and all things that they could rend above ground.

With Ulster more firmly subjugated than the other three Irish provinces it was decided to offer 500,000 acres of land to Scottish and English settlers who, it was stipulated, should be staunchly of the Protestant faith. That sectarian stricture passed bitterly down the years, dividing man from living man and breeding hate, fear and suspicion between the disparate tribes of an artificially troubled land.

The Irish tribes, robbed of land which they had held in common under the ancient Brehon laws, rose again in 1641, adopting some of the no-quarter tactics of their conquerors. They were defeated with the sort of unrestrained military ferocity that left large tracts of the country despoiled and reeking with the charnel house smells of genocidal slaughter.

Soldiers were instructed to kill all rebels, their families and supporters along with all men capable of bearing arms. They were told that 'nits will make lice' and urged to kill boys. That thought was to echo down the years, finding new expression in the colonial wars of the twentieth century.

Recent history shows that the British army has no monopoly on military terror, and it would be easy to put together a list of infamy, citing everything from the American atrocities against the civilian Vietnamese to the systematic brutalisation of a cowed and beaten Palestinian people by the Israelis. That would merely demonstrate the truism that the capacity for random savagery lies snugly in every soldier's knapsack, even in the most civilised of times.

The Golden Horde, which spilled out of Mongolia to carve a

bloody furrow across the face of the earth, were possibly less reprehensible in their ignorant savagery than General REH Dyer, a man who slaughtered hundreds of unarmed demonstrators for daring to assemble against his orders.

The Mongols had the excuse that they lacked the advantage of an English public school education. The massacre happened when Dyer ordered his soldiers to turn their machine guns on a 20,000 strong crowd in the Sikh holy city of Amritsar on an April day in 1919.

The state of Punjab had been simmering for some months as local political leaders rose to challenge Britain's right to rule in any part of India. As the agitation mounted troops opened fire on a small group of demonstrators, killing four people and transforming the survivors into a stone-throwing mob. Another twenty-five died in a second volley and, as the shooting continued, a wave of molten anger surged through the city.

The mob were in possession of the streets, mounting random attacks on anything British, whether it was people or property. The telegraph exchange was destroyed by a chanting, torch-bearing crowd of arsonists and a Scottish bank manager called Thompson was clubbed to death after he had shot and killed one of the rioters. The vengeful crowd found a cowering railway guard and beat him to death with sticks. A middle-aged missionary, Miss Marcia Sharwood, the superintendent of three church schools, was knocked from her bicycle and battered unconscious by a frenzied mob. That particular outrage against an English memsahib provided the main spark for the vengeful rage that was to grip General Dyer.

By the end of the first complete day of rioting Amritsar was in the hands of the Indian dissidents. General Dyer moved hastily from Jullundur with his troops, and immediately declared a state of martial law. Ten Indian ringleaders were arrested and chained to trees while Dyer ordered a tikitiki, a flogging triangle, to be set up halfway along the narrow, 150 yard long lane in which Miss Sharwood had been attacked. Randomly selected Indians, held by Dyer to be involved in the attack on the critically ill missionary, were taken to the lane and publicly lashed, as were the captured ringleaders.

The enraged general dismissed suggestions that, since the Indians were British subjects, they had a right to trial to determine their guilt or innocence. Since they were Indians, he said, they could not enjoy the same legal protection as Englishmen. His next move added to the tension in the city, stiffening the Indian resolve to continue their resistance to a military rule that was proving increasingly wild and arbitrary.

Dyer decreed that since all Englishwomen were sacrosanct the alley in which the missionary lady had been hurled from her bicycle was now a holy place. As a consequence all Indians who wished to pass through must do so on their hands and knees. Since the alley was crowded on both sides with densely populated houses many people were affected. Soldiers were posted to see that Dyer's orders were carried out. The soldiers added their own refinements by making the unfortunate Indians crawl upon their bellies through the muddy filth.

It was against this background of sadistic turbulence that a call went out for a massive peaceful demonstration with the joint purpose of celebrating a holy day and demonstrating the philosophy of non-violent resistance. Mahatma Gandhi told the people to leave the use of force to the British, adding:

> They believe in the doctrine of violence or brute force as the final arbiter. Our duty is to submit quietly to being arrested.

A huge, but peaceful, crowd made its way into the gardens of the Jallianwalla Bagh and, as some settled themselves to listen to the poetry recital which began the demonstration, others slept or played cards. Many people looked after the shoes of those who had gone to worship in the Temple. All of them were conscious of the fact that they were in the Temple gardens in defiance of General Dyer's martial law order forbidding their assembly. A small spotter plane, buzzing like an angry wasp, made swooping sorties above their heads.

Suddenly the bright air was full of the sound of thudding boots as an armed company of soldiers doubled into the square, taking up the kneeling position and aiming their rifles at the peaceful crowd.

Others positioned machine guns ready for open order firing. The crowd thought it understood the tactics, so it waited for the order to disperse. That order never came.

Instead there came just one word from the General: 'Fire!'

The machine guns opened up immediately and the riflemen started pouring in measured volleys. The soldiers were between the people and the gate. As people began falling before the hail of bullets the demonstrators realised with horror that they were trapped in a vast, three-sided box. There was blood, screams, shouts of anger, pleas for mercy, as panic-stricken people trampled on the dead and wounded in a rush towards a safety that did not exist.

Cordite smoke hung in the air, deadly black wisps of extinction. After a little while the soldiers had emptied their magazines, but Dyer told them to reload and begin again. He directed their fire up into the mighty peepul trees where some agile fugitives had sought safety. The bullets flew upwards and the bodies rained down like bagged pheasants.

A new order went out: 'In your own time, fire!' The soldiers were able to pick their own targets now. They concentrated on the people who were trying to climb the walls. It was an impressive exercise in controlled marksmanship. For an expenditure of 1,650 rounds of ammunition the soldiers had killed 379 demonstrators and wounded another 1,200. Some people had been hit more than once, so it was safe to assume that hardly a bullet was wasted.

When it was all over the local sahibs rushed to give General Dyer the respect due to a hero, but there were some annoying political implications. It was because of these, and much against the will of the imperial settlers, that Edwin Montague, the Secretary of State for India, was forced to relieve Dyer of his command. The general died a bewildered and broken man a few years later, having spent the declining time continually asking: 'Did I do the right thing?' It never was discovered whether his doubts were moral or tactical.

The grand moral gesture was left to another senior officer, General FP Crozier who commanded the 1,500 auxiliary policemen attached to the Royal Irish Constabulary during the 1916-1921 War of Independence. The auxiliaries, recruited exclusively from among former officers, were raised at the end of the First World War and sent to Ireland to combat the IRA.

General Crozier resigned his command during the campaign with the explanation:

> I resigned because the combat was being carried out on foul lines, by selected and foul men, for a grossly foul purpose, based on the most cynical of all rules, that the end justifies the means.

Contemporary chronicler Patrick J Power recalled:

> When the Auxiliaries had blood in their eyes they spared neither age nor sex. They were British officers, but not gentlemen. Fear-crazed drunkards many of them were, capable of the most fiendish cruelty.

On 1 December 1920 a group of auxiliaries arrived in Fermoy, a pretty little town in County Cork, on their way to the funerals of two lorry loads of their comrades who had been ambushed and killed by the IRA. Captain Nicholas Prendergast, an Irishman who had been wounded in both France and Italy while serving as a wartime officer in the British army, was the owner of the town's Blackwater Hotel. When Prendergast told an auxiliary who demanded to know if he supported the republican cause that he was an Irishman, the veteran officer was killed by a blow to the head from a pistol butt. His body was then dumped into the flooded Blackwater river.

Later the same night, when the drunken auxiliaries tried to start a dance at the town's Royal Hotel, they were told that a neighbouring shopkeeper, James Dooley, objected to noise after midnight. They broke into Dooley's shop, dragged the terrified man from his bed and threw him into the Blackwater river. They then took pot shots at him as he tried to swim feebly to the other bank. After that they moved through the town setting fire to shops and business premises and otherwise amusing themselves by horse-whipping men and lewdly insulting any unfortunate women they chanced upon, both verbally and by physical display.

Their outrages reached a peak on the night when they burned

Cork City. It happened on 11 December 1920 when the auxiliaries broke like a torrent of vengeance from their barracks, intent on evening the score for some spectacular IRA successes. Florence O'Donoghue, former adjutant to the Cork No 1 Brigade of the IRA, wrote:

> This was the most extensive single act of vandalism committed in the whole period of the national struggle from 1916 to 1921.

The frantic fire-raisers scorched their way through the city centre, burning shops, offices and houses and causing £3 million damage. Looting was widespread as the one-time officers ransacked shops and warehouses for anything saleable and transportable. General Crozier later said that one auxiliary stocked a shop in the north of England with goods he had looted in Ireland. During the carnage one group of auxiliaries went into a suspected IRA home and shot dead two brothers having pulled them from their beds.

All of this forms part of the rich military tradition to which Captain Nairac fell heir. That tradition embraces the untarnished heroics of a Lieutenant Pottinger as well as the demented antics of a Captain Nicholson.

The clinical efficiency of General Kitson's lessons in counter-insurgency also make their claim for attention and, since soldiering is essentially a slaughterer's trade, the butchery of General Dyer finds its place alongside the undisciplined savageries of the fifteen auxiliary companies sent to garrison Ireland. Maybe all of these combined to drown out the lonely voice of General Crozier calling out that the end does not justify the means.

Maybe Nairac heard that voice, but chose to ignore it.

We shall never know.

WARS ARE MOST likely to be fought by nations whose citizens are susceptible to lasting bouts of moral imbecility. Similarly, the sort of sustained belligerence that enables one country to plunder and dominate the territories of others, raises serious doubts about the mental and spiritual health of its people.

The necessary acts of conflict, shooting people down, blowing them up, poking holes in their bodies with sharpened bayonets, and worse, depends on the sort of destructive savagery which must surely spring from a psychotic disregard for the unique value of others. This dubious gift of madness is common, but for most men it remains dormant until some trigger causes it to erupt into aggressive life. It is then maintained at this level until whatever challenge caused its arousal has been dealt with.

The professional soldier is different. He does not go quietly about his business until some threat to hearth, home or country galvanises him into action. He adopts violence as a career, offering himself as a forged instrument of aggression in mindless pursuit of whatever policies his superiors may dictate. For such a man sanity may be the only aberration.

Captain Nairac belonged to this class of morally dispossessed automaton. He was driven by his own aggressions and possible need to court danger, and that may have led him to suppose that South Armagh in the twentieth century was broadly the same as India's north-west frontier a hundred years earlier. Poor Nairac discarded layers of sophistication and intelligence to indulge himself in an adolescent fantasy that lay shadowed by death, his own and that of others.

The urge towards violence was a constant factor in his life, and this is shown by his early forays into the boxing ring followed by his choice of a career which is ultimately about killing other people. There are those who claim that the magnet here was the need to demonstrate his own ambiguous manhood and, if that be so, then it is something he shared with the homosexual warrior Alexander the Great and the Second World War SAS hero, Colonel Blair Mayne, the Belfast lawyer who was also an Irish rugby international. He was a man whose military heroism rested on a degenerate framework of homosexual sadism.

Speculation about Nairac's sexuality is not really very interesting because, at the end of it all, he defined himself by his deeds rather than by his nature. He was a clever and educated man who lacked the excuse of many an unfortunate member of his class forced to seek a military career because of some restricting intellectual deficiency. Nairac's choice was dictated by his personality, and that to some extent was the product of his conditioning.

That conditioning eased him into a leading role as one of the armed enforcers of Britain's political will. As such he was absolved of the necessity of worrying about the moral niceties of his actions. He moved into a neutral zone where the only measure of value was whether a thing succeeded or failed.

He was serving his state and, although this is nowhere written down, it is widely understood that acts carried out on behalf of the state transcend the somewhat constricting notions of conventional morality. Even the most cursory reading of history shows that there is no infamy which a state will not commit in order to protect itself and its institutions. Nor is there ever a shortage of people to whom it can delegate such activities.

Captain Nairac, schooled by monks and taught the supreme value of free will, had effectively surrendered the right to make his own decisions, placing duty at the top of a pyramid of unquestionable choices. That sort of abdication does not lead to moral imbecility; it mostly occurs when the condition is beckoned in.

So Nairac, officer and gentleman, moved destructively across the Irish landscape, a man out of time, misplaced in history. All around him people were dying of a delinquent triteness that spanned the ages, submerging human values beneath a grossly deformed urge towards conquest and domination. Then Captain Nairac fell lifeless among them, finding a painful and trivial death on some inglorious field of dishonour.

It is only partly true to say that he died at the hands of a republican mob. What is more true is that Captain Nairac fell victim to a contagion of indecency, and that he himself was one of the carriers. Buddhism has a word for that sort of retribution. It's called the law of Karma, and it comes into play when a man suffers the consequences of his own bad actions. Christianity expresses the same thought in the phrase: As ye sow, so shall ye reap.

Out of the depths I have cried to thee, O Lord ...

5

The killers were waiting in the hedgerows. When they saw the lights of the musicians' bus breaking through the darkness one of them leaped out and started waving a torch, signalling the driver to stop. He held a sub-machine gun in his left hand and the muddy tones of his soldier's combat gear merged with the shadows of the surrounding night.

Two other men came on to the road as the minibus slowed to a halt. The rest of the armed men stayed hidden in the hedges. Their faces were black with camouflage cream and their stomachs fluttered with nervous anticipation. Some were entitled to the army uniform which they wore, others were not.

The three on the road moved quickly over to the minibus, pointing their guns and acting tough and aggressive. They had been called in for a grandiose paramilitary operation, an exercise in black propaganda that was soon to turn into a murder party. None of them knew that yet, so they spoke roughly and tried to put the frighteners on their nervous quarry.

There were five men in the minibus and they were returning to their homes in the south having played an engagement at a ball-room in the tight little Protestant town of Banbridge, a short half hour's drive from the border. Together the men formed the Miami Showband, one of Ireland's most popular musical groups and one of the originators of a rhythmic phenomenon that had been sweeping the country since the early 1960s. They had got as far as the small settlement of Buskhill when the soldiers spilled into the road, flagging them down.

The soldiers, swaddled in field jackets and with the green berets of the Ulster Defence Regiment carrying their own clear identification, formed a menacing cordon around the van. One of them reached in and snatched the keys from the ignition lock. Then he ordered the musicians out, telling them to stand at the side of the road, facing the hedge with their hands on their heads.

One of the soldiers, a civil sounding sort of man, asked the

Belfast born saxophonist, Des McAlea, how the dance had gone. It had been good, McAlea told him. The Castle Ballroom had been packed, and there were still dancers straggling around outside when the band left at about 1.45 am. Brian McCoy, the 33-year-old trumpeter who had been driving the minibus nodded in agreement.

'We love playing here. The greatest audiences are in the north,'
he said.

The man nodded: 'Aye, we're fond of a bit of good entertainment
when we can get it.'

Another man, wearing dark glasses and a moustache, growled:
'Don't be talking to these Fenian cunts. Get on with your job.'

He was the man who had flagged them down. Now he gestured
at them with a sub-machine gun.

'Don't turn around. Keep facing that field.'

As he spoke another man came out of the hedge. He, too, carried a sub-machine gun. The other men remained hidden. In all, ten of them had been mobilised for the operation. Two of them were to die and three would end up serving long prison sentences. The other five were to drift quietly back into the concealing security of their daily lives.

Suddenly there was a mighty blast and Des McAlea felt himself being lifted as though by a giant hand and hurled through the hedge into a field. He rose to a crawling position, feeling the minor cuts and grazes on his arms and legs, as he peered out through the tangled thicket of the hedge to where the minibus was blazing fiercely.

An English voice cut through the night, strong and authoritative,
giving orders. Then another voice, unmistakably Ulster, gave the
word to start shooting and suddenly the night was filled with the
deady chatter of gunfire. The voice belonged to a man named Mc-
Dowell. He was the one wearing dark glasses. He spoke again,
saying: 'Get them all. Leave no witnesses behind.'

The gunfire continued as the musicians slumped to the ground
and then twitched in agonised spasm as more rounds blasted into
their inert bodies. The voice came again: 'Okay lads, leave it now.
These bastards are all dead. The dum-dum bullets will have finished
them off.'

Des McAlea was the only member of the band to escape un-
scathed. He left behind a scene of reeking carnage as he crossed a
field and made his way to the road where he was able to hitch a lift
to Newry. Disbelieving policeman looked at him in horror as he
unfolded his tale of savage treachery.

Three of the Miami Showband musicians died that night, 31
July 1975. They were Fran O'Toole, the 29-year-old lead singer
from Bray, the small seaside town nestling at the foot of the Wick-
low hills. His corpse lay on its back, sightless eyes staring up at the
sky. There were twenty bullets in his body, most of them pumped
in as he lay dying on the roadway.

Brian McCoy also died as did 23-year-old Tony Geraghty.
They both lived in Dublin. Geraghty had been shot in the back, and
the gunman had continued firing a short burst of eight rounds as
the body slumped forward on to the ground. Stephen Travers, a
guitarist who had moved from Cork to join the band only six
weeks before, was wounded in the shooting. It took him several
months to recover from the dum-dum bullets, banned by international law, which had ripped through his body.

After it was all over, while grim-faced policemen scoured the
country road in search of bodies and bits of bodies, someone
picked up a lump of raw meat with the Red Hand of Ulster tattooed
on it. There was another tattoo which said 'UVF, Portadown'.
Those two graven affirmations of loyalist fervour were sufficient
to confirm that the bloody find was Harris Boyle's right arm. It had
been blown fifty feet away when the bomb he was planting exploded, killing Boyle and Wesley Somerville who was helping him
with the bomb. The rest of Boyle's badly burned body had been
blown in half

There was another body, blown apart at the trunk, some ninety
yards from the rear of the fragmented vehicle which had been
scattered in a radius of one hundred yards. Within the circle police
found a rifle magazine loaded with .32 ammunition, a .38 pistol, a
sub-machine gun, three UDR berets and a pair of spectacles. The
spectacles were to prove a uniquely valuable clue in leading to the
arrest of the Ulster Volunteer Force sergeant who McAlea remembered for his aggressiveness.

Among those watching as the grisly find was made was a member of the ambush party. Special branch officers recognised The Jackal among the ghoulish crowd that had gathered at the scene of carnage, and wondered what he was doing there. The Jackal was a planner, a top grade organiser who sometimes accompanied the foot soldiers on a blood and guts operation. He was not one of nature's spectators.

The special branch knew that he had been one of the three men who had neutralised John Francis Green. It was something in which they had no more than a casual interest. The killing happened outside their jurisdiction and the victim was a top Provo.

They knew, too, that Harris Boyle, a young gunman from Portadown with a violent urge to make a name for himself as a hard man, had been one of Green's killers. The Jackal used him like a clockwork toy, winding him up and pointing him at the target. Sometimes they wondered who held the key to The Jackal's motor. The answer to that is that more than one key existed. Captain Nairac, through his declared involvement in the Green killing, certainly held one of them.

The police heard later that The Jackal was at the scene of the Miami massacre to make his own angry assessment of a botched operation in which he had lost two valued men. He had made the plan, and been there to see it carried through. The men who whispered this to the police refused to raise their voices in a courtroom, so there was no possibility of putting The Jackal away. Other people went to jail, but The Jackal remained uncaged, buying his freedom at the cost of other men's fear.

Eighteen months after the massacre McAlea returned to Banbridge to give evidence at an inquest on the five dead men. Having described how he was blown off the road by the blast he said:

> I heard a lot of shooting which was automatic fire. I was very scared and I stayed as close to the hedge as I could. I wanted to make sure they all had gone before I went back on the road.
>
> I decided to make a run for it, and as I went I saw two bodies before me. One of these was that of Brian McCoy who appeared to be dead. The other was Stephen Travers and he was alive but could not

speak as he was badly shot up. I said I was going to get help and got
out over the hedge on to the road.

A pathologist told the inquest that the three dead musicians were
riddled with bullets. That fact provided its own proof that the gang
of unmasked ambushers were intent on leaving no witnesses.
Boyle and Somerville, whose cause of death was recorded as mis-
adventure, had been so badly injured that it was clear they were
either handling the bomb, or extremely close to it, when it blew up.

They had, in fact, been sliding a brief case containing a fifteen
pound gelignite bomb under the driver's seat when it exploded.
The bomb was supposed to go off after the musicians had crossed
the border into the Republic, blowing apart any trust that existed
between the British and Irish governments and reinforcing loyalist
fears that their southern neighbour was one vast arms dump for the
IRA.

Since the Miami Showband would have ceased to exist in the
blast there would be nobody to tell about the army patrol at Buskhill. It could then be safely claimed that the musicians, regular
cross-border travellers, were merely going home with a bomb
which they had failed to deliver to the IRA when it accidentally
detonated.

The plot failed because the desperate men panicked in the face
of a changing situation and allowed Stephen Travers to live and
Des McAlea to escape. That tends to suggest that if Nairac, the
SAS officer, was present at the scene he was there as an observer
rather than in a command role. The fact that an English voice was
heard at the scene has been confirmed by loyalist gunmen who
took part in the killing, but nobody had been prepared to link it to a
name. The most likely explanation for the voice is that the Miami
massacre was a Military Reaction Force operation, carried out by
loyalist gunmen on behalf of MI5.

BRITAIN WAS A country more savagely divided along class lines
than she had been for some considerable time as she slipped
angrily into the mid-1970s. The cosmetic egalitarianism that had

masked the deep social divisions in the country since the end of the Second World War were thrust impatiently aside as men with cultured voices began to assert their inalienable right to rule over those who dropped their aitches.

The country was in a state of ferment and revolution was in the air. This was a revolution with a difference. This time it was being mounted from the top.

There is the evidence of former agent Peter Wright, among others, that Britain's internal security service was then in the hands of a bunch of right-wing extremists whose aim was to destabilise and discredit the British Labour Party to such an extent that it would be incapable of forming another government.

Britain trembled on the brink of a military takeover and the north, the proving ground for counter insurgency techniques, played a vital role in the planning of the pin-striped supremacists as they went about their unmannerly task of staging a well-bred coup.

The spooks of MI5, desperate to seize control in the north of intelligence, handed to their rivals by Prime Minister Edward Heath in 1971, looked upon any weakening of six county links with the United Kingdom as yet another erosion of their power. They had a vested interest in keeping the British flag flying over the north and they were quite unwilling to allow a group of transitory, and reputedly subversive, politicians to interfere with their plans.

There is clear evidence that the spooks were playing dirty in the north at this period, manipulating not only bodies such as the UDA to their purpose, but actively masterminding a policy of selective assassination. It was in this that their chain of command extended to cover the activities of the armed counter-gangs and the SAS hit squads.

Peter Wright, the former MI5 man who wrote the whistle-blowing *Spycatcher*, which so annoyed Margaret Thatcher, tells of being introduced to a group of businessmen in 1974 who were anxious that Labour leader Harold Wilson should not be re-elected as prime minister of Britain. One of them said that the return of a Labour government 'could spell the end of all the freedoms we know and cherish'.

Those were days of rampant paranoia during which the sleek-faced men of the British establishment conjured up a succession of red bogeymen to account for the fact that their system had slipped out of gear and was plunging destructively downhill. Capitalism was in another of its periodic crises as a mocking and lingering condition of stagflation made a nonsense of every forecast. A moth-eaten economy mouldered away alongside a runaway inflation which drove prices through the ceiling even as it cut the value of money, shortened the order books and lengthened the dole queues.

There was alarm among the mighty. One captain of industry kept a ship moored in London's river ready to take him and his possessions to some safe haven when the disorderly rabble hit the streets.

Since those days the communist empire to the east has collapsed, and the grey and tired nations that emerged from its economic rubble have begun their tentative flirtations with the free market system. As they make their sharp, determined lurches to the fascistic end of the political spectrum the general assumption is that capitalism was right all along. That is not necessarily so. It was merely less inefficient. The time for the dancing of jigs has not yet arrived.

So, there was Britannia in the mid-1970s, a pucker-faced dowager living in a time of mounting civil disorder as people increasingly protested against the galloping destitution of the age. Times were hard and getting harder, and the old lady found she no longer had the power either to charm or command. In her hour of deepest need she found some unlikely, and abominably misguided, knights errant. One of them was Colonel David Stirling, the immensely tall founder of the SAS. He went along with the theory that the Red Menace was about to sweep across Britain.

Colonel Stirling had spent much of the 1970s working with the royalist forces in the Yemen as they tried to contain a popular uprising aimed at sweeping away the absolute monarchy that kept the country bound in the ancient chains of a corrupt and defunct feudalism. From this experience he concluded that these Arab chappies had a thing or two to teach the British. By May 1975 the colonel was back in Britain sending out a memorandum showing how he intended to save the nation from the socialistic abominations that threatened.

The memorandum went out to senior officers in all three armed services, leading industrialists, Intelligence chiefs and some members of parliament. It announced the formation of Stirling's private army, to be known as GB75 and solicited aid, financial or physical.

Stirling declared that the aim of Great Britain 75 was to defeat the left, inside and outside parliament, reverse Britain's economic decline and regenerate democracy. The organisation, which emerged at a time when various military and industrial leaders were setting up armies with the intention of staging a right-wing coup, saw strike-breaking as one of its more immediate roles, after which it would move on to confrontation with the other enemies of society.

After various leading Conservative politicians, fearful that the seething discontent that bubbled out of Britain's economic woes presaged a red revolution, had expressed doubt whether democracy could continue to survive, Colonel Stirling leapt into the fray with words of reassurance.

He told Martin Walker of the *Guardian* newspaper that he had been:

> approached very informally by some individuals recently who are very concerned about the appalling damage a major strike could do, interruptions of vital services like power, sewage and so on. It was the effect of the Ulster strike and the army's response to that strike, rather than the events of last winter's crisis, which caused their alarm.

The Minister of Defence, Roy Mason, condemned Stirling's proposals as 'blimpish bull' and a 'near fascist groundswell'. Stirling, who regarded Mason and his ilk as the enemy, claimed that GB75 was merely an organisation of 'apprehensive patriots'.

Stirling's mind turned to psychological warfare and he began making plans to demoralise Harold Wilson and his government by the use of various unpleasant and, it must be said, immature stratagems. He gathered together some former SAS comrades for a reconnaissance of the cellars of the House of Commons with the intention of flooding them with raw sewage from the heavily polluted River Thames. The plan fell through, possibly because the parliament was already overstocked with that sort of material.

In Belfast the MI5 overseer Peter England had drawn up a massive contingency plan to deal with any left-wing threat. It said:

> Another strike in Northern Ireland would require a flow of supplies across the North Sea. The mainland ports might be crippled by sympathetic strikes, and this would require the introduction of protective 'control zones' around them. Meanwhile terrorist attacks could be expected from groups like the Baader-Meinhof gang as British troops were withdrawn by plane from Germany. It would be necessary to guarantee their passage as well and that would require a 'control zone' around Heathrow airport.

British passenger liners, including the luxurious *Queen Elizabeth II*, would immediately be requisitioned by the revolutionary junta for use as prison ships for members of the deposed Labour government and other dangerous elements.

Now that all of this has passed into history it is possible to say that these ridiculous distortions of reality look like scenes from a pantomime rather than serious plans. It did not look like that at the time. There were mighty men then prepared to support these forays into political gangsterism. One of them was Lord Louis Mountbatten, the queen's uncle, and another was the newspaper magnate, Cecil King. He wanted to dispense with the elected politicians and draft in a group of 'practical businessmen' with Prince Philip, the royal consort, at their head.

It was possible to do this, the leaders of the various private armies said, because all oaths of loyalty related to the queen and did not extend to the left-wing rabble which happened to find itself in government. Nor, in fact, did it extend to any other government that might be formed.

In the north this piece of dubious illegality was seized upon by the spooks of MI5 and their military executives and by hardline loyalists who recognised in the new philosophy a way of circumventing the will of parliament should this prove unappealing.

THE MURDER OF the Miami Showband musicians served the
purposes of M15 in the north, since it aroused emotions on both
sides of the border and made it that much harder for the men who
sought some formula for peace to find any way forward. Seen from
that perspective the men who carried out the killings emerge as
sad, stupid and forlorn figures, creatures of the malevolent wills of
others.

It is not possible to place Captain Nairac among them, yet
there is forensic evidence which links him to the killing. The link
is forged by that Star pistol which was used at the Green murder.
Forensic tests showed it had also been used in the Miami slaughter.
It was the weapon which killed Brian McCoy.

Following reports of official alarm that the killers had been
masquerading as British soldiers, the Ulster Volunteer Force issued
a statement saying that the ambush had been carried out by its
members during a routine border patrol.

The statement said:

A UVF patrol led by Major Boyle was suspicious of two vehicles, a
minibus and a car parked near the border. Major Boyle ordered his
patrol to apprehend the occupants for questioning. As they were
being questioned, Major Boyle and Lieutenant Somerville began to
search the minibus. As they began to enter the vehicle a bomb was
detonated and both men were killed outright.

At the precise moment of the explosion the patrol came under
intense automatic fire from the occupants of the other vehicle. The
patrol sergeant immediately ordered fire to be returned.

Using self-loading rifles and sub-machine guns, the patrol returned fire, killing three of their attackers and wounding another. The
patrol later recovered two Armalite rifles and a pistol.

This ludicrous attempt to depict the five musicians as a mobile
guerrilla force, equipped with the sort of weapons needed to conduct a fire fight with armed soldiers, added that three UVF members were being treated for gunshot wounds. Despite the inference
that these had been inflicted in the gun battle with the lethally
armed Miami terrorists the statement did say that the men were not
in hospital, a happy circumstance which made it impossible to

check the claim.

Harris Boyle, the patrol commander, had risen higher within the UVF than in the UDR. The largest regiment in the British army, applying the standard tests of a regular military unit, assessed his leadership qualities as worthy of a corporal's humble stripes rather than a major's crown. Boyle, 24 and unemployed, benefited from a unique advantage he had within the UVF. He was The Jackal's personal hitman.

As such he was ready to kill anyone at his master's bidding, even a loyalist hero like Billy Hanna, home from the wars and basking in a reputation for gallantry. Hanna, who won the Military Medal in Korea, was a former B Special and now a part-time captain in the UDR. He marched to the beat of a staunchly loyalist drum. Captain Hanna was 45 years old on the night that his drum was stilled, not by a despised pack of misbegotten popeheads, but by a pair of true blue Protestants who feared that his fervour was beginning to fade. He was on his way home from a British Legion club in Lurgan where he had spent the evening reliving the glories of his military past with a bunch of other old buddies when his killers struck.

Captain Hanna recognised the two men who walked up to him as he stepped from his car outside his home. One of them was The Jackal and the other was Harris Boyle. The decision to kill Captain Hanna had been taken by The Jackal because the UDR officer's close ties with both the UVF and the UDA had given him a complete oversight on a good number of extremely sensitive operations. In particular The Jackal feared that Hanna might compromise the Miami Showband operation which was then being planned.

As the two gunmen walked up to the doomed officer he detected something menacing in their approach. He had never felt entirely easy with either of them, and there was a slight tremor of alarm in his voice as he asked: 'What are you playing at?'

The Jackal smiled as he lifted his pistol to Hanna's temple before pulling the trigger. Then, as Hanna lay on the ground, he bent to deliver the *coup de grace* with another shot to the back of the head. To this day Captain Hanna's distraught widow has been unable to identify the men who killed her husband, but the truly astonishing thing about this killing is that it happened while Hanna, suspected of playing a double game with the Loyalist gun gangs, was supposedly being watched by both the special branch and military intelligence.

That raises some tricky questions. It is quite understandable that a man under surveillance might fall to an assassin before his watchers could intervene. They would neither be geared up for, nor charged with, the task of acting as bodyguards, and so might easily be some distance away when the death attack occurred.

What is less easily understood is how the assassins could escape unhindered after killing a man who was supposedly being watched by both the army and the police. The surveillance teams would certainly have been armed, so any failure to engage the assassins would be puzzling. Equally puzzling would be a failure to give chase, since they would have been operating from a car.

If they were being watched the gunmens' escape takes on almost miraculous overtones when one considers that both police and army surveillance vehicles were equipped with radios. These could have been used to summon help. The area could have been sealed off and the men arrested.

The most astonishing fact of all is that neither The Jackal nor Harris Boyle was arrested at any time after the killing.

Now these were famous men, movers and shakers in the cause of Ulster unionism. Every special branch policeman in the South Armagh area was familiar with both their names and faces. They were both the subjects of mighty dossiers. Military intelligence knew them well. They were street heroes in the cause of militant loyalism and Boyle's later death was sufficient to cause a funeral pilgrimage from all parts of the six counties. Yet despite all this we are left with the incredible proposition that they were apparently free to kill a security suspect while he was under surveillance. That is just not believeable.

Surveillance teams are composed of men of comparatively junior rank who do not make policy decisions. What they do when confronted with armed men who are shooting is pull out their guns and start blasting.

There is one theory which fits all the known facts. The puppetmasters of Military Intelligence, alarmed by the possibility that Hanna might be about to blow a conscientious whistle on the Miami massacre project, and whatever other plans they were making to destabilise the threatening peace process, had been at their stealthy work. An order passed down at their behest to lift surveillance on Hanna.

This would not have seemed unusual. It would have been seen as another application of the standard military tactic of 'sanitising' an area by pulling out security units before an undercover squad goes in to carry out a specific operation.

If that theory is true the cancelling order in this case would have undoubtly come from high up the command structure and, since The Jackal was one of the killers, the suspicion arises that Nairac, who controlled some of his operations, was involved.

What is certain is that when the treacherous killers struck they did so safe from the gaze of the men who would otherwise have been watching the wavering Captain Hanna.

The assassination bore some of the hallmarks of a Military Reaction Force operation, so the theory must be given some credibility. Major General Frank Kitson had introduced the concept of the MRF to the north during his brief command of Belfast garrison in 1970. It had later been enthusiastically applied by Captain Nairac whose furtive role involved him in running turned paramilitaries who waged clandestine war against their former friends.

It is doubtful whether there were any British military recriminations over the death of Captain Hanna, although he was mourned in the messes of the UDR where his experience of actual miliary conflict gave him a certain rarity value. From the standpoint of a military undercover officer his death would have been perfectly acceptable. Dangerous men on both sides of the sectarian divide were there to be neutralised. A hardline loyalist paramilitary supporter who had not only infiltrated the UDR, but had got himself commissioned, might certainly be categorised as dangerous. It was a matter of timely efficiency for his own side to terminate him.

Boyle, who had built up an image as a local hero through his UVF activities, had come to the attention of the police in February 1973 when he was acquitted on a charge of unlawfully possessing arms and ammunition and stealing a car. That was the closest police came to getting a man they believed to be involved in violent activities that ranged from maiming and extortion to torture and murder.

His death in the Miami Massacre served to reaffirm everything the police, and his local community, had believed about him. Eight young women in the uniform of the UVF, which was then still legal, carried wreaths before the cortege as Boyle's body was borne from his home in Festival Street, Killicomaine to the cemetery. Ulster flags, edged in black, hung listlessly in the still air as bus loads of UVF members, brought in from all over the north, lined the funeral route.

There was a ceremonial farewell, too, for the second man who died in the Miami bomb blast. He was a 34-year-old factory worker called Wesley Somerville from Moygashel Park, Dungannon. Like Captain Hanna he was a former member of the sectarian police auxiliary, the B Specials. He was a part-time member of the UDR, and a lieutenant in the UVF. Three volleys were fired over his coffin by the UVF.

Along with his brother James, Somerville had appeared in court in 1974 accused of planting a bomb in a housing estate in Coalisland, Co. Tyrone, injuring a dozen Catholic residents, one of them a baby. The police case was that the brothers were members of a five-strong armed gang which kidnapped two baker's roundsmen and then used their van to deliver the bomb. Both brothers were acquitted.

There was to be no acquittal for James Joseph Somerville, a lorry driver's mate, when he next appeared before a court. This time he got 35 years for the Miami murders, having admitted he had also murdered Patrick Aidan Falls, machine gunned to death by the 37-year-old UVF man as he served behind the bar of a public house near Dungannon.

Thomas Raymond Crozier, aged 25, a painter and decorator of Queen Street, Lurgan, was also sentenced to 35 years for his part in the murders.

The patrol sergeant mentioned in the UVF release, James McDowell, was caught because he lost his glasses at the scene of the massacre. Acting on instinct a baffled RUC detective sent them to an optician for analysis – only to be told that they were of a type worn by only one person in half a million. A sweep through opticians' records turned up the name of 29-year-old McDowell who was a sergeant in both the UVF and the UDR.

McDowell was not, of course, a fulltime soldier. The man who was trapped by his spectacles earned his living making glasses for other short-sighted people.

6

The ship swept slowly into the lough, nudging past the gentle Antrim hills, and ploughing on towards her bleak landfall in the ragingly violent city of Belfast. It was high summer and the land shone beneath the falling sun, a patched mosaic that ranged from the burnt umber of harvested fields to the emerald green of rich pasture land.

Hillsides were dotted with small, miniaturised cattle, strays from a child's play set, and occasionally the thrumming, bee sounds of a working tractor floated out across the wide, rippling waters. The ship floated through a pastoral illusion whose peaceful surface was pitted and holed by the erupting turbulence that lay beneath.

Further down the lough, just where the weary city began its ragged crawl up the coastline, the colours ended and the world turned grey and drab. It happened suddenly, as though somebody had released a shutter separating light and shade. The murky, oxide-scented mist, the legacy of a booming nineteenth century, lingered ahead in the city air, the pungent memory of more prosperous days, another illusion in a city which lives by them.

Albert Walker Baker, a soldier gone missing from his regiment, came on deck and stood looking out to where the bow wave flecked a rolling white arrow of surf through the tumbling mass of the bottle-green sea. A light July breeze whispered against his face with pert familiarity as the black drink lay dying inside him.

Baker joined the Royal Irish Rangers as a private soldier in 1969. He had been a proud 19-year-old then, full of military swank and swagger, chest out, stomach in, ready to take on the world for the sake of England's queen and Dutch Billy's legacy of resolute Protestantism. Now, three years later, he was on the run and about to turn into the sort of vicious little sectarian killer who sought no greater justification for his killings than that the victim was a Catholic.

A generation after he went on his murder spree Baker was released from an English prison, seven years short of the minimum twenty-five year term which the judge recommended. That happened in the spring of 1992 and Ginger Baker, another man who discovered

100

God in a prison cell, went into hiding in Britain carrying the twin guilt of the killer-turned-informer into a nervously uncertain future.

It is a lifetime since he landed back in his native Belfast, watching the day make a slow surrender to night as he strolled comfortably past the rows of parlour houses which tumble down the canted hillside to where the mighty shipyard lies.

Since then the wheel has moved on. As Ginger Baker languished in his jail cell, sending out invitations to members of the press and various politicians to visit him in Albany Prison and other walled institutions that have held him, the tribute corpses continued piling one upon the other in his unforgiving homeland.

Shortly after Baker's release the total of dead victims of the 'troubles' passed through the three thousand mark, but that had nothing to do with Ginger. He finished his jail time in trim middle-age, fit and muscled from a dedicated exercise programme, a sinewy, born-again man, in touch with the Lord.

So, a God-seeking penitent nursed the knowledge of his savage guilt through the long, lonely years while the saving presence of a forgiving Christ slipped through the soiled fastnesses of the echoing jails to redeem the troubled soul of Ginger Baker. Praise be.

Yet it is only Baker's personal redemption that we are talking about here. The legacy of bitter and malicious hatred which he discarded has been chillingly adopted by a new generation of murderous evangelists whose beliefs are as yet unsanctified by any quality of mercy.

Ginger Baker, loyalist hitman, sectarian killer, retired, moves back into the mists of yesteryear, offering his penitent memories of a time of vicious carnage to the unfolding shadows.

Born-again and saved by the Lord, he's light years away from the surging blood-guilt of a merciless past, but it is still is only a flickering moment since he arrived back in Belfast to take up his role as a pitiless assassin.

THEY WERE IN a small room with a table covered by the flag of the Ulster Defence Association. There were other flags around the walls,

*the red, white and blue of the Union flag alongside the Ulster flag
and there were men standing around dressed in combat jackets and
wearing dark glasses. Some of the men carried small arms, pistols
and revolvers. They moved swiftly to attention when the three men
from the Inner Council came into the room.*

*Baker was there to take the oath required of all entrants into the
UDA. There was a Bible and a sword on the table and one of the
members of the Inner Council, Tommy Herron, administered the
oath. Herron, the leader of the UDA in East Belfast was both a
criminal racketeer and an unselective womaniser. He was murdered
after driving into the country with a woman for sex. His killer was in
the boot of the car. Security force involvement in his murder has
always been suspected.*

It was to Herron that Baker repeated the words of the oath:

> *Being convinced in my own conscience that there is a conspiracy to
> bring about a united Ireland by the use of force ... I will actively
> defend, by any and all means possible, the area under the control of
> the (UDA) Council.*

The oath carried an explicit warning to traitors:

> *Any betrayal on my part cannot be treated in a merciful way by the
> Council. I pledge myself to stand shoulder to shoulder with my
> Council brothers to face the enemies of my faith and freedom until
> death.*

For the embattled UDA, watching in alarm as its republican
enemies gave daily demonstrations of their ability to challenge the
north's catalogue of political and economic absurdities, Ranger
Baker was a considerable catch.

He had won prizes for marksmanship and then he was selected
for training in Texas with the US Army's gung-ho, bush-ranging
Green Berets, the meanest mothers in the jungle, the men who
pacified many a Vietnamese village by torching the dwellings and
murdering all its occupants. After the Green Beret experience
Baker went on to the SAS, the unit he was really with when he
staged his mock desertion. By now Ranger Baker was much more

than just another foot soldier; he was a member of Britain's growing band of Ninja warriors.

Even before he became a fictional deserter Baker had been
operating in Belfast. He grew his hair long and dressed as a hippy
and it was in that guise that several friends and relatives saw him
wandering around the loyalist districts of the city. One of these
sightings coincided with the arrival of a postcard which placed him
in the Arabian Gulf.

Baker was, in fact, serving with the Military Reaction Force
and living in the secret compound at Palace Barracks, Holywood.
In that role he formed a link in a chain that was later to include
Robert Nairac as part of its forging. Baker's first task was to re-
connoitre Belfast on the look-out for loyalist activists who might
be lured or coerced into a Kitson-style pseudo gang. That was all
to change after his supposed desertion, when he took on a far more
lethal role.

None of this came out at his trial when he was jailed for the
murder of four Catholics and a string of armed robberies. The
judge, who recommended that he serve at least 25 years, told him:
'I believe that but for the troubles in Northern Ireland you may
have continued to live a blameless and useful life'.

Before that, when the contrite Baker was pouring out his heart
to a series of detectives, naming names and trampling on the oath
he had taken by pointing an accusing finger at a succession of
UDA notables, the organisation made great efforts to distance itself
from the repentant killer.

Somebody had woken up to the fact that Baker had been plant-
ed on them by the army. He was happy to torture and kill Catholics
without a moment's thought, but he refused to fire on soldiers.
Somehow he managed to stay out of detention barracks when his
period of absence ended with him in military custody, although a
spell in military prison was almost mandatory in the circumstances.

None of this added up, and it was clear that Baker was a dubious and suspicious character. For the UDA men who were being
plucked from their beds by dawn police posses the realisation came
too late. By then Baker had not only used UDA resources in carrying out some gruesome terrorist murders, he had also plundered the

organisation of its most sensitive secrets.

AT THE START the meetings of the No 1 Assassination Team were held at seven o'clock every Monday evening on the guarded first floor of a small house in East Belfast, but then somebody said it was unwise to meet in the same place all the time because of security. The army and the peelers had eyes and ears everywhere and, if they got to know where the meetings were being held, they would put in bugs and then they would know every UDA move before it was made. Nobody wanted that to happen because some very sensitive matters were discussed at those meetings.

The team would get together and sit around the table while they talked over the names that were pulled out of the card index. Some of these were said to be very heavy Provos, and when a name like that came up there was an extra buzz of excitement in the air as the tactics for the stiffing were worked out. A lot of time would be taken up deciding on the best routes in and out of the nationalist area which sheltered the target, what sort of weapons to use, how many gunmen would be needed and where to steal the murder cars.

Some of the other names that came out of the index belonged to non-involved Catholics, people who had come to the notice of the UDA because they worked in Protestant areas or regularly travelled routes that made them accessible as targets. They were a bonus, and their names were added to the list because the strategy was to lay such terror on the Catholics that they would bow the knee in submission and reject their nationalist aspirations.

The graffiti on the loyalist walls, next to the murals of the Red Hand of Ulster and William of Orange triumphantly crossing the Boyne river having defeated the Catholic army back there in 1690, spelled out the message. 'All Taigs Are Targets', it said, making it clear that every Catholic lived beneath the gunman's shadow.

Within a month of joining the UDA Baker had established himself as one of the organisation's top men. His colleagues tended to be the sort of swaggering corner boys who would have drifted into backstreet thuggery even without an ideological justification. Baker was different. He was effortlessly professional, an instinctive soldier whose military talents had been refined by extra training.

The UDA warlords saw all this and pushed him quickly up the ladder, making him first a bodyguard for the members of the Inner Council, the important men who set objectives and directed policy. They had other uses for Baker's talents. Within a month of joining the UDA he had committed his first murder.

Philip Anthony Fay was a 19-year-old barman who had moved to Belfast from his native Cavan in the Republic in search of work. He was either unaware of the dangers that faced a Catholic in East Belfast, or he was too glad to get a job to care. When he was offered work in Holywood, a UDA stronghold, he eagerly accepted it. Not only that, he found accommodation in nearby Island Street.

Baker later told the English police: 'I used to go to the hotel where young Fay worked, just under the Holywood Arches on the Upper Newtownards Road where the UDA held their meetings. The Inner Council was in one room and Fay came in with drinks. Tommy Herron found that this geezer was a Roman Catholic and ordered his assassination in case he'd heard anything.'

The UDA party remained drinking in the hotel until closing time, after which Baker and another man who he did not name, went to pick up guns. They waited long enough to allow Fay time to get home and then, on 18 August 1972, they drove to his house and knocked on the door. It was after one o'clock in the morning and they waited in the dark street for Fay to answer their knock.

Eventually the door opened and Fay looked out: 'What do you want?'

Baker asked him: 'Are you a Roman Catholic?'

'I am so,' Fay said. They were the last words he uttered. Baker told him to turn around and shot him twice in the back of the head. As the young barman lay dying, Baker fired three more rounds from his .32 Browning automatic into the area below his ear. He told police he did that because the UDA said a target should always be finished off with a shot to the brain. Then, even if the victim survived, he would be a cabbage, incapable of making any identification or giving evidence.

105

Baker's statement added: 'I did not feel any remorse after that murder.'

Baker's next victim was also a barman. Paul McCartan was plucked from the streets of East Belfast as he rolled drunkenly homewards in the small hours of a morning just one month after Philip Anthony Fay had been murdered. His captors were Baker and another member of the UDA. They had been patrolling the Newtownards Road in their camouflage jackets and khaki slouch hats, looking for action, when they saw McCartan being let out of a police car.

An RUC sergeant said that the 52-year-old Catholic, much the worse for drink, had been offered a lift home, but had preferred to walk. The hapless McCartan, a shambling wreck who had long since lost any clear focus on life without a bottle, was to provide their sport for the night.

McCartan was taken to a premises which had a Romper Room. The name came from a local television programme for children, but the UDA's version of the kiddies' playroom had much more sinister overtones. Their Romper Rooms, mostly attached to loyalist drinking clubs, were used for interrogations and punishment beatings. For two hours McCartan was systematically brutalised and tortured before being taken away to be shot by Baker who, in a grim pantomime of a judicial execution, first placed a hood over his victim's head.

Baker later dismissed the death with: 'McCartan was nobody, just a Catholic. It was to keep the pot boiling, to frighten the Catholic community and the IRA'.

By now his appetite for sadistic violence was beginning to feed upon itself, so that he was no longer content merely to kill Catholics. Now they had first to suffer the extremes of pain before dying. This was a pattern of behaviour adopted by other loyalist killers who followed Baker. It reached its peak in the merciless cruelties of the Shankill Butchers who smashed into their victims with staves and iron bars until gobbets of raw flesh were scattered about the killing area. Pitiless brutality, inflicted upon the victim before death, became the hallmark of a loyalist killing.

Just a week after killing Paul McCartan the runaway soldier

chose another man with the same name for his next victim. James Patrick McCartan, aged 21, was out at a disco celebrating with friends who were to be married next day. As they left the disco Baker and some six other UDA men attacked the party and snatched McCartan saying: 'He's going for a ride with us. He's a Fenian bastard.'

The rest of the party, all Protestants, fought to stop the kidnap. The bride-to-be, Geraldine McCausland, was punched in the eye after she had shouted: 'You're not going to shoot him.'

McCartan, who was no relation to the unfortunate barman killed the previous week, was taken to a UDA haunt, Jones Club in East Belfast, where he was systematically beaten by nine members of assassination teams who had gathered for what had become a central feature in the UDA ritual of death.

When they grew tired of beating him with their fists they battered him with a wooden pickaxe handle until it broke across his back. After that he was held in the position of the crucified Christ while Baker stabbed him first through one palm and then the other.

Worse was to follow. With his captors holding him upright, McCartan's trousers were lowered as somebody suggested: 'Cut his balls off'. Baker moved around behind him, slicing a long, neat incision in the captive's left buttock. As the blood started McCartan's captors roped one hand to his ankles and threw the rope over a beam, raising him to the ceiling before dropping him on his head.

When they had enough of that Baker and several of the others took the sobbing man to a patch of waste ground and put a hood over his head. Then Baker shot him in the back of the head, making sure with another two shots up through the right ear.

Baker explained later: 'The younger McCartan was supposed to be in the IRA. This was information passed on by special branch and CID officers to a UDA commander'.

His last victim was a 46-year-old building labourer, Patrick Eugene Heenan. He died because he travelled on a work bus that followed the same route through a loyalist area of Belfast every day. Heenan was killed in February 1973, so Baker had been on the run from the army for at least six months when he committed that murder.

107

Heenan was one of twenty Catholic workers building a school at an exclusive residential development, Cherryvalley, in East Belfast. One morning as their bus slowed at a narrow stretch of the road a man on crutches hobbled out in front of it. Instinctively the driver trod on the brakes, bringing the bus to a stop. Another man rushed from the side of the road to smash one of the windows with a large, jagged piece of concrete. Ginger Baker followed him, lobbing a Mills bomb in through the shattered pane.

The blast followed almost immediately, tearing metal into jagged fragments and shattering the rest of the glass. Patrick Heenan died instantly and most of the other men were injured.

Baker told police that the UDA warlords were so pleased with this operation that one of them gave each member of the hit team £10 from the organisation's funds. That is the only record of Baker earning any money during his half year's service with the UDA, but he was certainly getting money from somewhere. There is solid evidence that he spent his evenings drinking heavily, so it is possible that he was taking a cut of the robberies he was pulling for the UDA. He would not have been allowed to take too much, though.

The UDA was largely under the control of greedy and brutal men who hid their gangsterism behind a facade of loyalism, men who used their sectarian ideology as a cover for enterprises of extraordinary criminality. Such men seldom err on the side of generosity. The most probable explanation of Baker's comparative affluence is that while posing as a deserter he was still drawing his soldier's pay.

It was partly Baker's unexplained solvency that started questions buzzing among the UDA leadership. That and the fact that they had heard he had been seen playing flower power hippy in Belfast while he was supposed to be fighting the Arabs in Muscat and Oman. Then there was the business of him being reluctant to shoot at soldiers at a time when the UDA was feeling sufficiently confident to take on the army in gun battles over the control of territory.

The Military Reaction Force had been in the news and the UDA chiefs began to wonder if Baker was a member. They were just about to ask him when he deserted the UDA and returned to the army, leaving behind a guilty trail of death and destruction.

Maybe he redeemed himself when, allegedly penitent and troubled in mind, he walked into a Wiltshire police station one afternoon in May 1973 and told Sergeant Anthony Godley that he was suffering from a bad conscience on account of the four murders and eleven armed robberies he had committed.

He had been reading the Bible, he said, and now that he had found the Lord he wished to unburden himself of the bitter anguish that crushed down on him. The Lord Chief Justice of the north, Sir Robert Lowry, believed everything Baker said about himself and sent him to jail for at least twenty-five years, but he was less keen to give credence to Baker's testimony on other alleged members of the UDA assassination team.

When that case came up Sir Robert acquitted the seven men Baker alleged were involved in the romper room murders.

Certainly the information that Baker gave to the security forces after he gave himself up was reliable enough to produce immediate results, including the arrest of one senior UDA leader and a dramatic rise in the number of loyalists accused of serious crimes in the following months.

During his prison term Baker gained a certain notoriety with his claims that he joined the UDA merely to further British policy by getting loyalists to murder and terrorise Catholics to discredit the IRA which would be seen to be too weak to protect nationalists.

Baker, who also told of his involvement with the Military Reaction Force, said too that he met his military handler, Captain Bunty, regularly in a Belfast city centre pub.

> We were operating for the UDA but we had close links with British Intelligence ... The guns we used were often passed on from RUC barracks, and nobody knew where they got them from .... Half of the assassinations in the early 1970s would not have been committed without RUC backing. They gave us files with pictures of republican suspects ... They even told us where to go to look for them ...
>
> There was a lot of people mixing in with the UDA and keeping quiet about it, but the politicians were most hypocritical. They would

set up a meeting with the UDA Inner Council who would hire a pub – the Bunch of Grapes on the Woodstock road – and the politicians would go there to the top room for their talks but they wouldn't go into the UDA headquarters or any other place that was under surveillance by the police ... I've had Unionist politicians so drunk I've had to put them over my shoulder, put them in the car and drive them home.

There is one baffling curiosity about the Ginger Baker story, and that is his claim that after his surrender he was visited in Belfast's Crumlin Road jail by the then junior minister for Northern Ireland affairs, William van Straubenzee. The minister was there, he claims, to arrange for his safety and that of his family after he had become the north's first supergrass.

Baker had, at that time, been making some dramatic claims that threw doubt on the democratic nature of Britain's government, while raising serious questions about how the rule of law was being bent into agonised deformities by security services which had lost sight of the fact that their main role is to guarantee the preservation of freedom. When asked about this alleged visit Mr van Straubenzee had an astonishing lapse of memory. He said it was all too long ago, and that he did not remember.

Political amnesia has often played a major role in Britain's dealings with her incredulous neighbour.

BY THE TIME Nairac arrived in the north to take up his undercover role the Military Reaction Force was running out of control and threatening to cause grave embarrassment to the military because of the openly murderous activities of some of its Belfast operatives. These were regular soldiers, and too many of them were appearing in court for a variety of offences revolving around claims that they were bringing indiscriminate death to the streets.

The claim was that they were riding around West Belfast and blazing away at IRA suspects from moving cars. The fact that none of the soldiers were ever convicted did nothing to lessen Catholic certainty that Britain had loosed a pack of killers among them.

In the ensuing reshuffle control of the MRF was firmly handed over to the SAS and Nairac was moved in to take up his Scarlet Pimpernel role as undercover SAS man and operational commander of an MRF field unit. That meant he not only gathered the information, but he then directed the consequent action. It was presumably this sort of dual role that placed him at the scene of the Green killing, and led to the suspicion that his was the English voice at the Miami Showband massacre.

The MRF was set up by General Kitson during his two-year tour of duty in the north in the early 1970s, but it was soon found that the techniques developed for fighting guerrilla forces in the African bush and the Malayan jungle did not translate directly to grey, wet Irish streets. Since closer control was needed over the activities of the pseudo-gangs, largely because of the fear of the disastrous publicity that might result from some of their wilder excesses, it was decided to put in some extra layers of supervision.

The SAS was charged with providing officers to train and lead the irregular force. Soldiers whose roots were in the north were recruited from various British regiments to provide a hard core of military expertise. In some instances, as in the case of Ginger Baker, these soldiers were given an enhanced role and sent out as undercover men with instructions to infiltrate target organisations. At one stage the UDA had within its ranks in Belfast some six alleged deserters from the Royal Irish Rangers alone. Strangely, they all returned to their regiment at about the same time as Baker.

The reformed MRF – whose members were known to their military handlers as the Freds – was moved completely out of Belfast because it was felt that its cover had been blown in the city, and because the IRA had started taking counter measures, like mounting road blocks in the areas under their control, making it certain that some MRF members would be captured if the operations continued.

There was another reason for moving. While a lot of space had been set aside in Palace Barracks to accommodate turned paramilitaries, recruitment had never matched expectations. There was the possibility that in dealing with the gentler, less abrasive type of man produced by the countryside, there might be more success.

The Military Reaction Force folded its tents and prepared to depart. A key SAS group, responsible for seeking armed confrontation with the IRA moved into Bessbrook Barracks and a combined SAS/MRF unit was set up at Ballykelly. It was disguised as a Signals Troop, a cover frequently used by undercover units. A third troop, the 4 Field Survey Troop, Royal Engineers, was established at Castledillon. This was the one Nairac was to join. A lot of blood was spilled before he got there.

BY THE SUMMER of 1972 Seamus Wright was so confident that he was getting away with his bluff that he increased the time he was spending away from the small house in Leeson Street, West Belfast where he lived with his young wife.

Wright, in his early twenties, was a would-be playboy with a taste for easy women and the sort of ten-pints-and-a-fish-supper night out which he confused with fulfilled living. He was a member of Belfast's 2nd Battalion of the IRA and he fell prey to British Intelligence one day when he was lifted off the street and taken to Castlereagh Holding Centre where he was told the special branch had enough evidence to send him down for an IRA murder. To buy his freedom Wright gave up the names of every member of the battalion's D Company, a unit which had been both active and successful in the Lower Falls area of West Belfast.

From Castlereagh he was moved into the compound in Palace Barracks and recruited into the MRF, part of 39 Infantry Brigade which was then commanded by Kitson. There was not much fraternisation between the loyalist and republican Freds, he later told his IRA interrogators. Mostly they kept to themselves, avoiding the company of former enemies. Later the role of the Freds was to be extended, but at that time they were mostly used for low level surveillance work, travelling through the ghetto areas lying flat on their bellies in the back of an armoured car while an army photographer took pictures of the men and women they pointed out.

Wright's absences from home, periods when he was in the compound either training for his MRF role or out on a spying mission, was explained by a carefully concocted cover story which placed him in England looking for work, or actually working. The IRA became suspicious of these absences and pulled him in for questioning. Just as Wright, a lukewarm republican married into a staunchly nationalist family, had cracked before his Castlereagh interrogators he now broke down under questioning by the Provisional IRA.

He gave his interrogators a detailed report on how the MRF operated, explaining how his indepth debriefing had started with close questioning about his childhood and the people he had known as he grew up before going on to explore the present day. He had been shown albums of photographs and asked to point out and name republicans.

Sometimes he would be shown film of IRA funerals and asked to identify the mourners. At other times he toured nationalist areas in an armoured car, pointing out republicans on the streets to the army photographer who travelled with him. It was against this background that the Provisional IRA made the decision to spare Wright's life on condition that he started working for them against his British masters.

Wright, a born opportunist who was to show a surprising talent for working a double bluff, eagerly fell in with the suggestion. The Provos gave him low level information – such as the location of a few expendable rounds of ammunition – to pass on to the MRF and kept a record of what he told them, building up a fat file on the Reaction Force and its methods of operation. He also passed back information about the people involved with the MRF.

A wave of shock swept through the Provisional's intelligence gathering wing when Wright named one of the turned operatives he had seen in the military compound as Kevin McKee, a member of the Provisional IRA from a family whose contribution to the cause of republicanism earned them the respect of their neighbours. He was related to one of the founders of the Provisional IRA and the record of his family's involvement with the nationalist cause went back over several generations.

Wright claimed to have seen him swaggering around the MRF compound wearing a pistol in a shoulder holster and getting the sort of friendly and admiring treatment from his handlers that suggested he was something of a star player. It took forty-eight hours of concentrated interrogation by the Provisionals before McKee broke, and even then it did not happen until he was confronted by Wright. By this time both men were under IRA arrest

McKee disclosed that he had been taught by the army how to work effectively with a whole range of weapons, although he pretended ignorance of why the army should take that much trouble with him. His interrogators did not need him to tell them he had undergone the standard training programme for a man who was to be used as a killer.

Satisfied that he would kill no more, the Provisional questioners were more interested in what he had to tell about an MRF operation known as the Four Square Laundry. This was cover for a van which toured West Belfast picking up dirty washing which was tested for evidence that it had been near explosives or someone who had fired a gun before being cleaned and returned to its owner. The van travelled with two soldiers lying in a secret compartment in the roof which provided them with both a view of the terrain and a comfortable position for taking photographs.

Two offices, one of them used as a massage parlour in North Belfast and the other serving as a reporting point for the van crew in the south of the city, were also revealed as MRF operations. On 2 October 1972 the IRA shot up both offices as well as ambushing the laundry van.

A military policewoman, Lance-Corporal Jane Warke, who had been going from door to door collecting laundry, showed remarkable presence of mind in making her escape. As the van came under fire she sought shelter in a house, claiming that loyalist gunmen from the Ulster Volunteer Force were trying to kill her. One soldier was killed in the three concerted attacks, and another man wounded.

McKee and Wright were taken down to the border territory in South Armagh, hooded and dispatched with the traitor's bullet to the back of the head, and then secretly buried. As a mark of the IRA's detestation of informers their bodies were interred in unconsecrated ground.

For the shell-shocked and battle weary people of West Belfast, under constant threat from wandering gangs intent on burning down their homes and driving them from the area, events took a new turn on 22 June 1972. Undercover soldiers started shooting at people from unmarked cars.

Three men were waiting at a bus terminus in Glen Road when there was a burst of fire from a civilian car. Two of the men, Joseph Smith and James Murray were injured and another man, Thomas Gerard Shaw, was hit by a stray bullet which came through the open window of his bedroom as he lay sleeping in a nearby house. Peace moves were being made at the time and the incident came as an interruption to the continuing truce talks.

Sergeant Clive Graham Williams, a 26-year-old member of the MRF was charged with attempting to murder the three men at the bus stop. He had been in civilian clothes, said the prosecution, when he had opened fire with an automatic rifle from the rear window of his Cortina car. Williams denied the charges and claimed that one of the shot men had been carrying a carbine, and the other had been armed with a revolver. They had fired six to eight shots at his car, he said, with one of the rounds smashing through the rear window. Only then did he return fire.

Mr Brian Hutton, prosecuting, told the court that the three men were not carrying weapons and that tests on Sergeant Williams' car suggested that the rear window had been knocked out deliberately, rather than smashed with a bullet. Forensic tests indicated that none of the men at the terminus had fired a weapon, since there were no residual lead deposits on their hands. He also said that having shot the men Sergeant Williams, who described himself as the commander of a unit of the Military Reaction Force, drove away without attempting to recover the alleged terrorist weapons. Nor did he summon military assistance.

Williams told the court that there were some forty men in the MRF and that he had been returning from the rifle ranges where he had been demonstrating the use of a Thompson sub-machine gun to some new recruits since, he said, this was a weapon favoured by terrorists. The normal issue weapon for the unit was either a Sterling sub-machine gun or automatic pistol. As he drove his recruits through West Belfast the Thompson was concealed in a holdall.

That was because he feared that if other soldiers saw a gun in his car they would open fire upon him and kill him.

Williams was acquitted of all charges. Earlier charges relating to the unlawful possession of a Thompson sub-machine gun and ammunition had been dropped against Captain James McGregor, another member of the MRF, who had been travelling in the car with Williams when the shooting happened.

Suspicion of MRF's role deepened with the gunning down of a group of vigilantes, drawn from the Catholic ex-Servicemen's Association, who were on patrol in the Andersonstown area of West Belfast to guard against random sectarian killings and infiltration by fire-bombers. As the unarmed group stood watchfully on the pavements a car drew up alongside them and Patrick McVeigh, the 44-year-old father of six children, fell dead as a burst of machine gun fire ripped into him.

All the other five vigilantes fell wounded as the car made a screaming three-point turn and roared off towards the neighbouring Protestant enclave of Finaghy. Astonished witnesses saw the car drive away after stopping to produce identification at an army checkpoint.

Having first said that the killing was apparently motiveless the army admitted that the shooting had been done by undercover soldiers. There was the usual claim that the shot men were carrying rifles and revolvers and that they had fired first. Once again the forensic evidence showed that none of the vigilantes had fired weapons. The inquest returned an open verdict, attaching no blame to anyone for the killing, but the coroner made the suggestion that the shooting may have been started by two vigilantes who had then fled the scene. No soldiers were called to give evidence.

Martin Dillon in his book, *The Dirty War*, documents several cases of MRF activities in West Belfast, an area which the formation targeted for priority action. Dillon details the case of Gerry and John Conway who were attacked as they walked down to the Falls Road to catch a bus.

A car screeched to a stop alongside them and three fit-looking men dressed in civilian clothes leaped out with pistols in their hands. The Conway brothers turned and started to run back towards their home, but fell as bullets bit into them. As neighbours gathered to offer assistance to the wounded men one of the gunmen made a radio call from their car. Shortly afterwards two armoured personnel carriers arrived and there was a consultation between their occupants and the gunmen. They all left the scene as the shot men were transferred to the Royal Victoria Hospital.

The British army later claimed that a mobile patrol had been fired on by one of the Conway brothers who dropped his pistol and escaped after the patrol returned fire. The British army alleged one of the men was on the army wanted list, and the other was a suspect. Despite these claims neither of the brothers was ever charged which is strange since there would certainly have been fingerprints on the discarded gun. For some odd reason this does not seem to have been recovered by the undercover squad.

Another MRF attack that went wrong happened in the exclusively Protestant Shankill district when a mobile patrol opened up on a car carrying four people. The driver sped to the nearby Tennant Street police station to claim they had been attacked by the IRA. Somehow the army vehicle managed to crash, trapping its undercover crew inside.

They had to be rescued from the raging mob by their uniformed colleagues. A search of the military vehicle revealed that the soldiers were equipped with nylon masks, a strange piece of equipment for a supposedly legitimate force. Once again the army's explanation was that the occupants of the car had started the shooting.

That left a slight inconsistency. It was puzzling why these desperate characters should first try to massacre a group of soldiers and then immediately drive into a police station having, during the short car journey, managed to rid themselves of their alleged weapons along with all traces of ever having fired them. Curious, that.

7

The gadfly left-wing politician Ken Livingstone stung the British House of Commons out of its somnolent pomposity when he departed from tradition and used his maiden speech to dart a series of accusations at the deplorable Mrs Margaret Thatcher. He claimed that she knew all about her country's dirty tricks campaign in the north as it was going on.

Livingstone, the newly-elected Labour MP for Brent East told a packed chamber that Prime Minister Thatcher's friend and adviser, Airey Neave, killed by an Irish National Liberation Army car bomb in 1979, was in close contact with the group of MI5 officers who, Livingstone said, were behind the Miami Showband massacre and other counter-terrorist atrocities.

He also named Captain Robert Nairac as the most likely organiser of the massacre. The MP's claims, made on 8 July 1987, followed an investigation he carried out with the assistance of a full-time researcher. During the investigation Livingstone conducted taped interviews with witnesses who had first-hand knowledge of British intelligence operations in the 1970s, either as officers in the security forces or members of military-backed loyalist gun gangs.

Livingstone, former leader of the Greater London Council, called for an enquiry and said:

> As long as the Prime Minister continues to resist this – and she was the main beneficiary of the traitorous officers in MI5 – any reasonable person can only come to the conclusion that she was kept informed in some degree via Airey Neave, who had close links with the security services.

Britain's intelligence services had spent a considerable part of the 1970s fighting a multi-layered campaign. Firstly they were battling each other for supremacy, and alongside that the extreme right-wingers of MI5 were plotting to re-establish the ruling classes as the political leaders of Britain. Both of them were fighting in the north, using its torn terrain as a ready-made arena in which to display their tactical skills. They were playing games, but these games needed bruised and battered victims, along with a sad supply of broken and lifeless bodies.

They found one of their victims in young Columba McVeigh. He was a simple-minded youth of 17 whose skin-deep republicanism was worn more for its fashionable cut than for any reason of thought-out belief. He paid with his life for the careless barbarity of combative men. British security set him up and the Provisional IRA knocked him down.

McVeigh's troubles began on an autumn day in 1973 when he was scooped up in Dungannon, Co. Tyrone, by a military patrol which was out on a trawling mission. Under this system arrests were made at random, mostly of youths in the troublesome fifteen to twenty age group, so they could be taken into a police station for spot interrogation. For the RUC, and the British army field intelligence NCOs who worked with them, the tactic brought a considerable yield of usually low-grade intelligence. Occasionally it produced a golden nugget.

The Military Intelligence Corps sergeant on duty at the RUC station, when McVeigh was brought in, thought he had made a golden find after a short conversation with the boy. The sergeant, trained to find the weaknesses in other people's personalities, realised that McVeigh was putting up a facade of truculent bluster to hide a nervous and uncertain timidity. He started working on that.

Little by little he chipped away at McVeigh's professed republican beliefs as he slowly persuaded the youthful captive that his best interests would be served by working for British intelligence. The sergeant had been nurturing a daring plan for some time. He made a serious misjudgment when he decided that McVeigh was the person to carry it out.

The sergeant and his RUC colleagues were anxious to nail a local priest whom they suspected of running the Dungannon end of an IRA escape route for wanted and wounded men. They were also anxious to trace the supposed route, and to see if it was possible for a fugitive to infiltrate the IRA as a recruit so that he could later pinpoint training camps and the people who ran them. Alternatively cowed by threats of imprisonment on drummed up charges and bolstered by promises of reward, the hapless McVeigh agreed to go along with their plan.

To establish credibility with the Provisional IRA, increasingly conscious of security because of the number of informers who had bored their way into the fabric of the republican group, McVeigh was given a cigarette packet containing three rounds of ammunition. This he was to leave in his bedroom where it would be found when the security forces staged a dawn raid on his house.

He was told to be away from home for the search and, having found out about it, to make all the nervous, fidgety moves of a man on the run. The raid was carried out by soldiers who did not know they were playing a role in an elaborate charade. That is why, when they failed to find McVeigh, they put his name and description on to the list of those wanted for questioning.

After that things started to go badly wrong for the unfortunate McVeigh. The supposed runaway made contact with the suspected IRA priest and told him he was a wanted republican. Maybe somebody had fingered the wrong man, or maybe the priest was suspicious of the gawky teenager. For whatever reason, he told McVeigh he could do nothing for him and sent him on his way.

With one avenue of infiltration blocked off McVeigh decided to make his next call on another priest known for his republican sympathies. That is when he found that sympathy is one thing, active participation another. The priest did not approve of IRA violence and had no pipeline into the organisation. Once more a worried McVeigh was thrown back on his own meagre resources. He could think of only one thing to do, and that was to make contact with the man who had cast him in the Judas role.

He walked into the police station and asked to see the Intelligence sergeant. Seconds later his arm was up his back as a jubilant RUC constable shouted out that he had bagged the wanted terrorist, McVeigh. The neophyte spy, increasingly feeling himself the victim of malign circumstance, was kept in the cells overnight until his army controller came on duty. Then he was surreptitiously released.

McVeigh was still roaming aimlessly around the streets a week later when another army patrol picked him up. Left, right, left, right, pick your bloody feet up, Paddy. This time he was charged with possession of the ammunition and there was no way he could be freed without compromising the plot. The arrest had taken place in daylight and too many people had seen him being scooped into the back of the military vehicle.

The resourceful sergeant then decided the best way to deal with the situation was to exploit it. He instructed McVeigh to follow IRA tactics by refusing either to plead or recognise the court when he came up for trial. The unfortunate youth was consigned to trouble when he was remanded to Belfast's Crumlin Road prison and lodged in the wing housing republican prisoners.

The word had been passed in that McVeigh had no connection with the IRA and had never even been a member of its youth wing. There were some people on the outside anxious to know why he had adopted IRA procedures when he appeared in court.

It took just one beating in the shower area to make the frightened teenager confess his dealings with the undercover British sergeant, but that was not enough for his fellow prisoners who had convinced themselves that he must have more information to give. In desperation McVeigh came up with a list of people he said were informers.

There were two appalling facts about that list which was to cost five lives. The first was that all the names were false. That was to lead to the death of an innocent man. The second fact, even more nauseating, is that the coded letter containing the names which the IRA smuggled out of the prison was intercepted and deciphered by the army which then did nothing to warn those named of the dangers they faced.

The evidence for that comes from Major Fred Holroyd who saw the decoded letter while going about his duties as a military intelligence officer in the Dungannon–Portadown area. Among those named in the letter was a solicitor, a politician from the constitutional nationalist SDLP and the McVeigh's milkman.

On a cold February day in 1974 two masked IRA men loomed out of the morning gloom to shoot and kill Christopher Mein, a 29-

year-old Protestant, who was doing holiday relief for the Mc-
Veigh's regular milkman, the one named in McVeigh's letter.
Three Catholics then died in reprisal shootings by loyalist para-
militaries. That was four dead.

Before that happened McVeigh was back before the court
which took the unbelievable course of giving him a suspended sentence. So far as the court was concerned McVeigh had behaved
like an IRA man and might, therefore, be presumed to be a member of that group. No IRA man accused of possession had ever
drawn a suspended sentence.

A local priest, Father Denis Faul, said the court's decision was
'tantamount to a death sentence'. It certainly indicated to the IRA
that McVeigh, with his cover blown, was of no more interest to the
British who were prepared to release him on to the streets to meet
whatever fate awaited him. McVeigh fled to Dublin where he lived
with his brother for a year. Then the IRA picked him up for what
they call a Bord na Móna job, named after the state-run turf recovery agency.

McVeigh was executed and buried in a bog some thirty miles
north-west of Dublin in the flat plains of County Meath. His was
the fifth death to result from a ruthless attempt to force a weak-
witted boy into a role for which neither nature nor intelligence had
fitted him. McVeigh, a trusting youth, as unselectively approving
of others as an excited puppy, was lured out of the cosy candy-
floss world of his own limited perceptions, first to be frightened by
the threats of imposing men and then to be stirred to greed by the
promise of reward. Because of that he died.

*FORMER BOXER JIMMY O'Hara went down for a count of seven
after he walked into a garda station in Monaghan town and demanded the release of his two kidnapper mates. The Lisburn fighter was
acting on the belief that all the gardaí were part of a plot to snatch
IRA suspects and deliver them back across the border to the British
army. Unfortunately for Jimmy he'd got that bit wrong, and the result
was that he finished up in a cell with the other two muscular
loyalists.*

The British attempt to use O'Hara and his broken-nosed buddies as a Fenian retrieval squad was fraught with disaster from the start. In March 1974 they were offered £500 to go to Monaghan and bring back Eamonn McGurgan, a known republican who was wanted for questioning. The offer was made by an army officer, later identified as Captain Nairac. He told the pugilistic threesome that a highly-placed mole in the gardaí would make sure the area around McGurgan's house would be frozen, with no gardaí or other security presence there.

All the boxers had to do was knock McGurgan on the head, tie him into a sack and dump him back over the border where he would be accidentally found by a military patrol. There was high drama before the kidnappers took to the road because the promised £500, which they wanted in advance, did not arrive.

Urgent representations were made to MI6 supremo Craig Smellie to tap into the clandestine funds used to finance unattributable operations. Smellie, who once asked Major Holroyd if he would be interested in doing some bank robberies to boost the secret funds, put the money together in used notes and it was then handed over to the Cauliflower Ear Squad.

The three contenders then set off for Monaghan in an old Ford car which was stopped at an army checkpoint before they reached the border. Somebody had murdered an Irish politician in Castleblayney, they were told, and there was a major alert all along the border. The boxers were instructed to return to base where, to their considerable disgust, they were required to hand back their £500 purse money to Mr Smellie.

Two weeks later they were offered a return match, promoted by a member of Nairac's team. This time their targets were to be Seamus Grew, whose later death in an RUC special unit ambush sparked claims of a shoot-to-kill policy, and Patrick McLaughlin. They were briefed by an SAS sergeant who gave them maps and photographs of Grew's house on the edge of Monaghan town and a sketch of the area in which they were to dump their trussed-up captives. Once again £500 changed hands.

Jimmy O'Hara's two sidekicks suffered a technical knock-out when he sent them off to case Grew's house and see how they could get in and out. They lurked so furtively that several people called the gardaí to say that two suspicious and clearly criminal types were loitering around the neighbourhood with the undoubted intention of committing some sort of rascality.

Half an hour after taking up their vigil they were behind bars, vainly trying to persuade some disbelieving country cops that the sacks they carried were most certainly not for removing whatever swag they might come upon in the course of their planned house-breaking expedition.

The matter was clarified when Jimmy O'Hara strolled amiably into the garda barracks to declare in strangulated Ulster tones: 'Youse wans have made a tarrible mistake. Yis'll need to be letting my wee men go till we do the job we came to do.'

The garda behind the counter looked at him with polite interest. 'And which wee men would these be now?' he asked, knowing that there were only two men being held in the station.

'The wans youse lifted outside Seamus Grew's house.'

'Ah yes, I see. The burglars.'

Which is how Jimmy O'Hara and his sparring partners were put down for a count of seven.

When they went for trial in Dublin they were each given five-year jail terms, a judicial haymaker which left them sagging on the ropes and challenging the ref's decision. The heavyweight bruisers of the Appeal Court added another two pulverising years to each of their sentences, tapping home their mastery with a dazzling display of forensic fisticuffs.

THE SEARCH BEGAN for Senator Billy Fox early in the morning of 12 February 1974. He was the Irish politician whose murder had halted Jimmy O'Hara and his team in their first kidnap incursion. The hunt began after a gang of armed and masked men took over a house Fox was visiting. They held the family at gunpoint and then burned the house to the ground.

Fox, a 35-year-old member of Fine Gael, was elected to the Dáil in the 1969 election. The seat had previously been held for years by James Dillon, one of the party's founders who later became its leader. The 1973 election saw Fox losing his seat, but being appointed to the senate as one of eleven new members.

The attack happened at the home of Richard Coulson, a farmer of Tircooney, which lies about three miles from Clones on the Monaghan road. The farmer's son, George, lived with his wife and two young children in a caravan near the house. That was also burnt out. Searching gardaí later found Senator Fox's car parked in a laneway about one hundred yards from the farmhouse, but there was no sign of the missing senator. Mr Coulson and his wife, strong country folk but elderly, were taken to hospital to be treated for shock.

Mr Coulson said later:

> I was sitting in the kitchen with my wife, my son George and my daughter, Marjorie. A friend of ours, Billy Fox, was also there. About twelve armed and masked men rushed into the house and said they were looking for arms. They ordered all of us to lie down on the floor.
>
> They tied the hands of my son George behind his back as he lay on the floor. They then ransacked the house, searching upstairs and downstairs and throwing everything about. After that they piled all the furniture together and after ordering us outside they set the house on fire. I heard a shot being fired outside my house. I have not seen Billy Fox since. The men ran off across the fields.

Twelve hours later Fox's body was found hidden behind a hedge in a field two miles from Clones. The discovery was made at 10 am but a full day was to pass before the corpse of the dead man was removed because of the fear of booby traps. The postmortem examination showed that he had been shot twice, once in the chest and once in the hand. They were the sort of wounds a man might receive while trying to escape.

The arson attack and the murder of Senator Fox presented some unusual features for the investigating team. At first sight the atrocity had all the hallmarks of a loyalist operation, but both Fox and the Coulsons were Protestants, part of a prosperous enclave that had remained to work the rich lands that lay along the border with the north.

As detectives were pondering this enigma a telephone caller, describing himself as Captain Wilson, a recognised code name used by the Ulster Defence Association, said that Fox had indeed been killed by loyalists. He had died while resisting questioning by the Ulster Freedom Fighters, the assassination wing of the UDA, the caller said. Despite the fact that Fox was a Protestant the UDA believed he was linked with the IRA, the caller claimed.

That theory gained some credibility when Ruairí Ó Brádaigh, President of Sinn Féin went on record to say:

> The late Senator Fox was active in protests against the British army actions in cratering roads, firing CS gas and rubber bullets across the border and making incursions into the 26 counties. He was also engaged in efforts to find a political solution to the present conflict and secure a lasting peace. In the course of this work he became known personally to Republican leaders ...

The IRA then weighed in with a statement denying any involvement in Senator Fox's murder and adding rather querulously:

> We have repeatedly drawn attention to the murderous activities of a group of former B Specials led by serving officers of the British army which has carried out a number of attempted assassinations, burnings and bombings in the Clones area in the last few months.

Nobody was listening, or if they were, they were not listening hard enough. What the IRA was describing was the make-up and activities of a unit of the Military Reaction Force, but since the claim came from the paramilitaries it was ignored.

Senator Fox, it turned out, was the victim of a poisonous bigotry that exactly mirrored the loyalist creed that all Taigs are targets. It was unfortunate for Senator Fox and the Coulson family that they should be professing Protestants in an area where some, steeped in their own wash of brutish ignorance, regarded such a faith as the infallible mark of an actively calculating traitor.

Rumours had been circulated that Fox once belonged to the

hated B Specials. Other stories said that the Coulsons were using their house as an arms dump for loyalist gangs. All of this was lethally untrue.

Quite early in the investigation the claim by Captain Wilson of the UDA that loyalists were responsible for the crimes was discounted. A lot of people knew about Captain Wilson and his coded calls and the garda concluded that the confessional telephone call had been made to distract them from the real culprits.

These, they were convinced, were republicans. That did not necessarily mean the arson and murder had been committed by the IRA, but with the chaotic command structure around the Monaghan area at that time it was quite possible that some members had mounted an unsanctioned operation. That, in fact, is what happened. Ten men were pulled in, all known republican sympathisers, and later five were sentenced to penal servitude for life for their part in the offences. They had burned the house and caravan to destroy fingerprints after their search.

ONE DAY IN 1974 an IRA informer told Major Fred Holroyd, a career officer whose faith in the virtue of the army's role in the north was about to come under sustained attack, of a plan to shoot a policeman on the following Sunday.

The weapon to be used, a rifle, was appropriately hidden in a graveyard in Lurgan's nationalist Kilwilkie housing estate. The soldiers had developed their own mythologies about the savage hordes of Fenian psychos who roamed the wild Kilwilkie terrain. They told each other: 'Don't go in there, chum, they'll tear the bollocks off you. And that's only the women'.

Like Nairac later, Holroyd was then reporting to the MI5 chief, Craig Smellie. Smellie asked for the top rounds from the clip of ammunition so that he could arrange 'to give the chap a bit of a surprise'.

Holroyd's field intelligence NCO, Sergeant Bunny Dearsley, took the rounds to Smellie who had them filled with detonator explosive. The IRA killer would have his head blown off by an exploding rifle as soon as he pulled the trigger. Holroyd, alarmed by these unorthodox tactics, took the matter up with his brigade commander who cancelled the operation. Instead he sent Holroyd to sabotage the rifle's firing mechanism so that when the hidden sniper opened up on the policeman the gun just clicked ineffectively.

That perceptible lack of ruthlessness was what finished Holroyd in the end, bringing him to a hospital where they said he would be strapped to a stretcher and sent back to England if he did not toe the military line. That happened after he had got involved in an internal tussle between MI5 and MI6. Since then he has made a lot of claims that do not reflect well on the British army.

At the same time he lives under the stigma of a man whose mental health was once called into question. Yet the facts are that he was not dismissed from the army on health grounds. He resigned in protest three months after having been forcibly taken to a mental hospital. The record of that hospital stay has since been expunged from his military medical record. Allegations that his wife and family were in danger from him have since been withdrawn.

It has been argued that Holroyd, a disaffected man, has coloured the facts of his experience in the north to bring discredit upon the British army. It might be equally well argued that Holroyd, a conscientious man whose sense of honour has been outraged, has exposed the practices he saw because he believes there is no place for them in the army of any civilised nation.

Holroyd was born in Ashington, a mining village in Northumberland where the bitter north-east wind blew a flecking of coal dust across the laundered fronts of the little houses, giving them a fine, black veneer. The coal-house was outside and so was the lavatory. He lived there with his grandmother who kept a tin bath hanging on the back wall, taking it down nightly to wash the grime from him. That was his mother's side of the family. His father's side, who were comfortably off, lived in Harrogate in Yorkshire. He moved there in 1946 when he was four years old.

By the time he joined the Royal Artillery in the ranks at 18 he had been through grammar school where, as a member of the combined cadets, he developed a passion for soldiering. Five years after joining the army he became an officer and was posted to Malaysia. He did not altogether approve of what he found there.

He tells of his experiences in his book *War Without Honour*.

> The British officers I met in Kluang badly let the side down. Given
> too much time on their hands, they often behaved in a grotesque cari-
> cature of the worst type of colonial overseer. An excessive social and
> drinking life, rife with affairs, made me ashamed of my uniform at
> times. I also became aware of the pervasive influence of Freemasonry
> in such circles.

In an early manifestation of the streak of solid Yorkshire puritan-
ism, which was to stir again uncomfortably in the north, he asked
to leave the unit before completing his two-year tour.

By 1973, with fourteen years soldiering behind him, Captain
Holroyd was training to serve as a military intelligence officer in
the north.

> What I didn't then know about the war I was about to enter was how
> the rule of law and order was not what it seemed, and I would en-
> counter illegalities on my own side that would severely dent my
> sense of purpose. I understood there was a certain mood of ruthless-
> ness pervading our thinking on counter terrorism ...
>
> At the time this was going on I was 100 per cent behind it. I
> would have gone with Nairac and helped him to do the killing. We
> were highly motivated, fighting a ruthless enemy ...
>
> But I have become a victim of them. They stuck me in a mental
> hospital and refused to hold an enquiry into what I was saying. These
> people are a law unto themselves. There may be times when you have
> to break the law and play these dirty games, but it should be author-
> ised at the highest level.

By the early 1970s the Intelligence men running covert actions
against the IRA had given up any pretence of operating within the
cumbersome framework of a law which demanded that offenders
be arrested, tried and convicted only after a telling weight of evidence was presented against them. For these accomplished killers
the due legal process was far too slow. They much preferred
assassination to arrest.

One of their more spectacular victims was Eugene McQuaid, a

motorcycle enthusiast from Newry. McQuaid, who was married with five children, was not a member of the IRA, but like many another in that area he was ready to perform the odd service for the republican movement. He was doing one of these errands when Felix the Cat blew him to pieces.

The countdown to death began for 35-year-old McQuaid on a mellow autumn day in October 1974 after a farmer had stumbled on some rockets hidden on his land to the west of Dundalk. After he told the gardaí, who then called in an army officer, a labyrinth of entrapment and deceit arose around the murderous cross-border connivings between individual members of two legally constituted bodies.

After an Irish army officer had made a report to his superiors a request arrived through secret channels that a team of British explosive experts should be allowed across the border to covertly inspect the cache. Permission was given. In the event only one man, an explosives officer, crossed to look at the rockets, called bombards by the British army. They were of a type which had previously been used successfully against armoured vehicles in the north, and with a range of some eight hundred yards they posed a formidable threat.

The officer who crossed the border took the opportunity to do more than just look at the bombards. He sawed through the safety pins, making the rockets unstable and likely to go off with careless or rough handling. The assumption was that they would explode as soon as somebody touched them, killing the person who came to claim them and frightening a few farms animals. It did not work out quite like that.

Two days later Eugene McQuaid uncovered the cache and strapped three of the defective rocket warheads along with their launchers and a timing device alongside the petrol tank of his motorcycle. Then, skirting Dundalk, he rode carefully up the main road between Dublin and Belfast, conscious of the explosive nature of his cargo but not really aware of its deadly menace. He got as far as Killeen, just below Newry, when he ran into what looked like a normal British army checkpoint and did a swift turn to head back across the border. That is when he died.

McQuaid had been under surveillance from the moment he had left the cache but the gardaí, unsure of the effect of stopping a motorcycle carrying rockets, had been forced to let him run. The British army, alerted to his progress by continuing radio calls, were able to prepare for him. They set up an unmanned checkpoint, and dug the soldiers in a long way back from the road. The aim was to halt McQuaid before he could get to Newry which, like Dundalk, was packed with Saturday shoppers. A pair of snipers crouched ready to blow him off his motorcycle as he slowed.

They had no need to fire. There was a mighty roar as the rockets exploded, fragmenting the motorcycle into hurtling lumps of shrapnel. McQuaid died with sudden mercy as ragged segments of his body rained down over a radius of hundreds of yards. Lumps of bleeding flesh hung from the recoiling branches of a quivering tree. A swift, total silence wrapped itself around the scene as birds fell mute and the idle murmurings of the country faded into reflective stillness.

An attendant from a nearby petrol station came running to the scene to find McQuaid's severed head, still wearing the dead man's helmet, lying at the foot of a tree with a thin line of blood trailing gently from the nose. His torso, burst at the belly by the direct blast from the rockets, lay nearby. The pump attendant watched in disbelieving horror as one of the soldiers walked over to it and pulled out a handful of entrails. He held them aloft for his mates to see.

'That's the end of another of you bastards,' he said, looking up at the bloody, dripping mass.

That was his way of marking the triumph of Felix the Cat, a symbol used by the British army's explosive disposal teams and its intelligence units. His superiors found another way to celebrate.

Holroyd records that he visited Brigade headquarters in Lurgan while the army was clearing up after the motorcycle explosion. He found a group of Intelligence officers and the Brigade's explosives officer, who had primed the rockets, in a jovial mood.

> They were sitting around, guffawing like a lot of schoolboys in the tuckshop. The big jar of white mints they kept to celebrate successes

in the field was being passed around to mark the killing of Eugene McQuaid.

Explosives also featured strongly when a mixed army and RUC team blew a driverless train off a bridge on to a Catholic area. The aim was to discredit the IRA, who had removed the driver, by causing the maximum damage around Portadown's Obins Street.

Just three days before Armistice Day, as the north's loyalist population prepared for the ceremonies to commemorate the dead of two world wars, a group of army and police officers met in an RUC station to consider the case of the runaway newspaper train. Among them was Captain Robert Nairac and his commanding officer, Captain Julian Ball who was on secondment to the SAS from the King's Own Scottish Borderers.

A gang of Provos had stopped the train north of Dublin and put off the crew. They had then tied down the controls so that the train would hurtle non-stop at 100 miles an hour through the night. Police feared that it might be carrying a bomb, and that when it hit the buffers in Belfast it would cause major damage to the commercial heart of the city.

The suggestion that the train should be blown on to the small Obins Street community after it rounded the long sweep through Portadown was made by an engineering officer who spotted that this stretch contained the longest bend on the entire route. The chosen point was in the Tunnel area, a Catholic enclave in the hardline loyalist town. This huddle of houses lay beneath the elevated rail track. There was always the possibility, the engineering officer said, that the speeding train would jump the rails of its own accord, but in case that did not happen several officers left to lay charges on the line.

Shortly before the train was due to reach Portadown there was a mass movement to the station by the assembled officers, all of whom had now agreed to go ahead with sabotaging the train. They met an unlikely but decisive opponent to their plans in the shape of Mr Robert Milne, the signalman on duty. Mr Milne, a dedicated railwayman, had been searching for a way of handling the situation so as to cause the minimum amount of damage to the runaway train and anything it might hit. Now, he believed, he had found it.

While heedless officers listened with mounting impatience to Mr Milne's plan to divert the train into a siding where it would do comparatively little damage, the speeding runaway was roaring towards them, lurching and swaying through the night with a rattling menace. Mr Milne started to detail his plan again, and continued to do so until he was ordered from the signal box and escorted out by armed soldiers.

The train roared into the long curve, plunging across the points where the signalman had hoped to divert it, and leaning over mightily as its wheels screamed their way around the seemingly endless bend. Then slowly and majestically, it was toppling off the rails and tumbling towards the small, terraced houses in Obins Street.

Metal shrieked in twisted agony as the huge locomotive gouged its way off the track and slid slowly towards the houses, a monstrous juggernaut that threatened to tear the heart out of the small community.

Somehow it never happened, and those who know about such things talk about the decelerating pull of intrinsic inertia and the braking effect of a frictional contact against a moving mass whose tail outweighed its falling head. Others speak more simply of a moment of grace. The locomotive came to rest on the bridge, lying on its side, groaning in agony like a wounded dinosaur.

The RUC later acknowledged officially that the train had been blown off the track because of the danger that it might have hit Belfast. They did not say that Obins Street, with the enthusiastic participation of a group of British army officers, had become the chosen spot for derailment. Nobody ever explained why the train was not blown off its tracks on one of the long country stretches along the route.

8

Saturday night, hollow-eyed from small debaucheries, staggered on towards the chaste primness of a shining Sunday morning, and so the story ends where it began, with a broken man waiting for death's easeful release.

Before that happened the men with blood in their eyes had set their killing machine in motion.

Liam Townson, the third eldest of nine children, was standing at a bar counter in Dundalk when the two men came for him. He'd been on the drink all day, but he was holding it well. When they told him to get a bit of hardware because there was a man who needed shooting he nodded and rolled after them into the car.

Townson fled the north when somebody dropped the word that the peelers were truffling around the area, trying to pick up his scent. The police wanted to ask Townson, a 24-year-old joiner from the small village of Meigh in County Armagh, about his involvement with the IRA, and three killings. Townson, the ultra-republican son of a British soldier who settled in Ireland, slipped over to Dodge City and found work as a labourer on a farm near Dundalk.

Behind him he left a family which was well-respected in their local community. Townson's mother was a nurse and his father a health inspector who was also a church organist.

Now Townson was driving through the night on a murder mission. As Townson was first taken to a house to collect his gun, and then on to the killing field, the brutalisation of Nairac continued as another attempt was made to dupe him into making a false confession. The Belfast court heard a statement from one of the accused men which said that Terry McCormick, the man who sent for Townson, leaned over him, murmuring: 'You can talk to me. I'm a priest'.

That sparked a renewed attempt to escape which resulted in Nairac getting another severe beating. Somehow during the struggle the false priest, McCormick, got shot. As McCormick whispered his Judas words, Nairac surged to his feet and tried to make off across the field. Instantly they were all over him, pulling and punching, kicking and gouging.

Another captor, Pat Maguire managed to fire the captured officer's 9mm Browning, putting a bullet through McCormick's side. It

*ploughed through the flesh just above McCormick' hip, leaving clean
entry and exit wounds.*

*One man who had been sent off to move cars away from the
Three Steps Inn so that nobody would know their owners had left
without them returned to the killing field and parked his car at the
gate. He told detectives later that by the time he returned most of the
kidnappers had left.*

His statement, read to the Belfast court, said:

The other boys were away. Then I heard them talking somewhere
around the middle of the field. When we got to where they were Liam
Townson was there. He had the gun and was hitting the soldier over
the head with the side of it. He was asking the soldier about the Stick-
ies in Dundalk. The soldier was lying on the ground, on his back or
his side. Townson was kneeling beside him.

While I was watching Townson hit the soldier on the head about
four or five times. He was laughing while he was hitting the soldier.
The soldier had his hands over his head, but did not speak. He beat
the soldier for about five minutes and then he came to where we were
all standing ...

Townson said to the rest of us: 'I'm taking this fellow over the
fields to shoot him'. I then saw him get the soldier up off the ground
... they had only gone a few yards when I heard Townson shout that
the soldier had got the gun.

Incredibly, Nairac had made another attempt to get free.

The evidence continued:

Pat Maguire ran up to where they were, and we all ran up behind him.
Kevin Crilly and Terry McCormick then turned and walked down towards the gate. I saw Maguire get a thick stick from the ground and
start to hit the soldier over the head with it. The soldier was down on
the ground at this time. When Pat Maguire stopped hitting him I noticed his face and head had a lot of blood round them.

The witness said the stick was 'about four feet long and as thick as
your arm'.

His statement continued:

I then saw Townson point the gun at the soldier and I heard the soldier ask for absolution or to see a priest. Townson then said to him that he had time to say a prayer ... About a minute after this Townson pointed the gun down at the soldier and pulled the trigger. It was aimed, I would say, at the soldier's head. The gun made a click but did not go off.

Townson said, 'Fuck you, it's only blanks'.

One of the accused men, Thomas Morgan, stated:

He kept pulling the trigger and after about four clicks the gun went off. The barrel was about two feet from the soldier's head when it fired. When the gun went off I turned and walked towards the gate.

Townson and Pat Maguire came down the field just behind me. They were talking and Townson was laughing.

I heard Maguire ask Townson if he was sure the soldier was dead, and I heard him say that he was dead because he knew by his eyes. Down at the gate they were all talking and Terry McCormick asked me if he was dead. I said he was. Townson told me to say nothing about the shooting. I then got in my car and left ... I got home about 2 am.

Next morning, he said, he went to 10 o'clock Mass in Dundalk and then again an hour later to Mass in Jonesborough. He met Danny O'Rourke there and they set off for the Border Inn to relive the excitement of their night of savagery over a couple of loosening pints. O'Rourke had travelled in Kevin Crilly's car to fetch Townson from Dundalk.

We met four men who had been with us the night before in the kidnapping ... We said the body should be moved over to the north that night to keep the Free State out of it. The following Monday or Tuesday I met one of the men and he told me that the body had been taken care of.

FUCK YOU IT'S only blanks. Forgotten pagan gods were crawling out of their timeless chasms, reviving old furies in this murderous field beyond the edge of Armagh county, a place of sacred death where massacre and mysticism imprint their timeless memory on the

136

very stones.

The soldier said: 'I know you are going to kill me. Please. I need to confess. Get me a priest'.

It was difficult to see in that darkness but when the man said 'I am a priest, you can talk to me', Nairac turned away from him. Bubbles of blood slipped from the corner of his mouth to leave a faint tracery of suffering as they slid slowly down his chin.

Out of the depths I have cried unto thee, O Lord:
Lord, hear my voice:
Let thine ears be attentive to the voice of my
supplication.
If thou, O Lord, shall observe iniquities: Lord, who shall endure it?
For with thee there is merciful forgiveness: and by
reason of thy law I have waited for thee, O Lord.
My soul hath relied on his word; my soul hath hoped in
the Lord.
From the morning watch even until night: let Israel hope
in the Lord.
Because with the Lord there is mercy; and with him
plentiful redemption.
And he shall redeem Israel from all his iniquities.

In the City of Armagh there are two cathedrals. They sit less than half a mile from each other, in the midst of hills that are spiky with electronic listening posts, military watch towers and other strange artifacts of an age that wears technological obscenity as a latter-day mark of the beast.

Both cathedrals, listening posts of another sort, are named for St Patrick. The one belonging to the Church of Ireland has been rebuilt around a mediaeval core. In its Chapter House there are the statues of old, redundant gods, stony reminders of an earlier paganism. The roof and walls of the Catholic cathedral are covered with pictures of usurping saints and angels.

Just two miles west of the old city the legendary Queen Macha has left a huge pre-Christian legacy in the mighty ceremonial enclosure of Eamhain Macha. The old royal site of the kings of Ulster had served its purpose for eight hundred years until it was destroyed in 332 AD. Its name has been Anglicised into Navan Fort, but as the original Ard Macha, Macha's Height, it gave Armagh it name.

It is all around, this mix of paganism and Christianity, potent and volatile, a heady cocktail that threatens the susceptible with a bout of spiritual insobriety. Tensions, taut as harp strings, stretch between the old, permissive pagan culture and the implantation of an increasingly austere Christianity which finally, in a spirit of righteous uplift, cut the links which held the two systems in some sort of tolerant balance.

The responsibility for that lies mainly with the scholarly St Malachy, a Primate of Ireland, who was born in 1095 in what is now Ogle Street, Armagh.

He inherited the See of Armagh at a time when the tolerant Irish clergy had adapted Christianity to suit the needs and temperament of their inattentive flock. They did this largely by ensuring that the average humble sinner did not need to concern himself over much with religion, a circumstance which appears to have worked to the satisfaction of both parties.

A monastic system had developed, which meant that much of the praying and other religious observances were carried out by a body of religious specialists. It was this class of dedicated spiritual intermediaries which gave Celtic Christianity its ascetic character, along with the social cohesiveness that developed around the religious settlements.

St Malachy altered all that. At a time when a series of blackguardly popes were starting to lay the groundwork for the Protestant Reformation with their cupidity, corruption and unbridled licentiousness, the Armagh Primate abandoned the Celtic tradition and, by adopting the Latin rite, brought the Irish church under the dominion of Rome.

There was a rapid tightening of religious discipline as the duties and nature of laymen were now curtly defined: 'They are of two classes, husbandmen and warriors. Their duties are to attend church, to pay first fruits, tithes and oblations, to avoid evil and do good, and to obey their pastors'.

Less than thirty years later Pope Adrian IV celebrated the inclusion of Ireland within the papal domain by giving his written blessing and approval to an invasion plan by King Henry II of England. His successor, Alexander III, ratified the conquest in 1171 and was then paid a one penny tax for each household in the country. That set the pattern for the pillaging future.

Armagh, the holy city of sacramental carnage and its troubled hinterland, have presided over the funeral rites of many a broken man as ravaging waves of Vikings, Normans and native Irish pillagers have cut their savage swathes across the flinching fields.

As the Dark Ages settled on Europe, spreading a blighted ignorance all around, there was a flowering of scholarship in Ireland based on the monasteries which quickly established themselves as centres of wealth and learning.

From the barren ice lands to the north, fierce waves of Vikings set out in search of plunder. They left behind homelands made desperate by harsh winters and widespread starvation to sweep down on Armagh and other Irish settlements, slaughtering those who dared to resist their uncontrolled orgy of rape, robbery, murder and pillage.

The gentle monks were taken as slaves while the gold and silver which adorned the churches were carried off, along with whatever other ornaments might be discovered.

For almost two centuries each new generation of Armagh citizens was to endure at least one of these terrible visits. In the years between 831 and 1013 the Norsemen returned at least ten times to remove the new wealth from the settlement, to put its fighting men to the sword and to select male slaves and concubines from the rest. Under one of their leaders, Thorgeis, they occupied Armagh for more than four years.

With Viking power broken by Brian Boru at the Battle of Clontarf in the early eleventh century a power vacuum was created around the cathedral city. This was filled by the O'Neill clan who scattered terror all around as they battled rival lordlings for control of the fertile lands. The O'Neills mounted their forays from a fortified stronghold in Dungannon, but the military superiority they had established was soon to be broken as an even more ferocious gang of landgrabbing cut-throats took to the field.

These were the Anglo-Normans who came storming into Ireland in 1169. Their belief that killing an Irishman was a matter of no more gravity than dispatching a dog seems oddly at variance with the supposedly evangelising nature of their papally-blessed mission. Their coming introduced the hapless Irish to the dubious but lasting notion that the morality of the mailed fist is superior to that of the naked hand.

Armagh was caught in the middle as the battles between the contending armies raged across the countryside. Eventually the invaders, by a combination of terrorist methods which included torture, massacre and imposed starvation, subdued the dissident natives. By the time they had achieved their victory so much hurt had been inflicted on the land that its people did not rise again for two hundred years.

History was being written in the blood of a sacrificed nation as the edifice of Norman power rose steadily on the stricken corpses of its victims. Weakened and subdued by a series of murderous raids, the city of Armagh became once again a sanctified slaughterhouse in which the gentle prayers of pious men were drowned beneath the agonised wailing of the butchered and dying. Chapel and charnel house, the anguished city continued to fulfil its dual role as host to blood-crazed men who cut down the meek, and humble ones who died uttering words of forgiveness.

The dissolution of the monasteries, with their subsequent spoliation by military bands who had discovered the redemptive ecstasy of looting for the greater glory of a reformed God, brought a new outbreak of fighting. By now the Celtic nobility were too weak from the long centuries of continuous warfare to offer any effective opposition to the colonising armies, so they fled the country.

That ended the old order and left the way clear for King James I to commence the Plantation of Ulster in 1608 with his Scottish army whose religious faith has often seemed to be more firmly based on a hatred of Catholicism than on the love of Christ and their fellow men. They marched to the rhythm of religious discord, and the sentiments they brought with them have slipped poisonously down the years to provide a chant for their descendants:

Slewter, slaughter, holy water,
Harry the Papishes, every one,
Tear them asunder, and put them all under,
The Protestant Boys will carry the drum.

A deal had been struck in which brutal intolerance became a major weapon in attempting to impose some sort of political stability upon a recalcitrant land. It did not work because the uncultivated Irish, used to holding land in common, were unable to distinguish between an irreproachable act of Royal land expropriation and the commission of a massive theft.

It was this cynical confluence between religion and politics which, in 1795, led to a development that has bedevilled the history of the north ever since. The Protestant settlers who lived around County Armagh at that time became fearful that their Catholic neighbours would combine against them. They set up a secret society, called the Peep O' Day Boys from its tactics of rousting the native Irish from their beds at dawn on the pretext that they were searching for arms.

Their fear and trembling, which was possibly explicable as the natural nervousness of those who found themselves in illegal possession of a disaffected neighbour's property, was a mere ploy. The real purpose, freely admitted by many members of this lawless band, was to so intimidate Catholics that they would flee the county, swelling the army of dispossessed vagabonds tramping the roads.

Since there was then no means of enforcing law and order, beyond relying on the goodwill of neighbours, the Catholics set up their own protection group called the Defenders. After several skirmishes the Defenders and the Peep O' Day Boys met in open battle. Despite claims that the Catholics were armed, forty of them died while just one Protestant was killed. That is either a splendid tribute to superior Protestant marksmanship or an indication of their partial approach to the facts.

Later that night, at a farm belonging to Dan Winter, a new secret society was formed by men who were alarmed by the strengthening Catholic will to resist the daily oppressions that were being visited upon them. The new society was the Orange Boys which time was to transform into the Orange Order, the mightiest political weapon in the Protestant armoury and, until the abolition of Stormont in 1972, the real government of the north.

For the beleaguered nationalists the feat of political legerdemain which stripped the Unionist-dominated legislative assembly of its powers made small difference. They still lived as second class citizens in an occupied land that was held down by armed, alien force, suffering higher unemployment with its consequent poverty and deprivation than their Protestant fellows.

The killing still went on, as it had for centuries, with death piling on wasteful death until it came the turn of a British undercover officer to die in a field surrounded by a gang of baleful drunks who hooted with malicious glee to see an enemy brought low.

The figure of the compassionate Christ, or any of the other icons of regenerate man, had no place among the lurching destroyers in that field. The night shone with ebony hues as the dark angel of death looked down on the condemned man, another casual offering to the perverted hungers of a ravening history that had taught men to devour each other.

Yet there was here a place for the old Celtic gods, the spirits of river and forest who lacked familiarity with such concepts as mercy and forgiveness. They crept out of the past, summoned by blood-red rage, spectral shadows that stirred wild, jubilant memories of conscienceless destruction. Or did they?

It is fanciful and dramatic to say that they were present, filled with atavistic malice and the impassive cruelty of those who lack a sympathetic imagination. That would be a comforting thought, but it can exist only as a poetic hallucination. These gods were illusory, totally unreal.

They sprang from neither wood, river nor field. They were there only because they had been summoned from the darker recesses of men's minds, the hidden crannies where the lurking shadow of original sin, the predisposition to evil, lies on a bed of moral psychosis.

In a way those men in the field represented one of the great dilemmas of our times. It is more than a century since Nietzsche,

an underdeveloped little fellow who thought that a race of super-
men was about to be born, announced that God is dead. Since then
the rest of us, acting in concert and by common consent, have dis-
posed of the Devil. In doing that we managed to destroy our ultimate alibi.

A dead Devil cannot tempt anyone, so the only thing to be said
is Yes, it was us. We did it, all on our own and of our own volition.

We have moved into a world of stark truths in which everyone
is their own cloven-hoofed tempter. The satanic fall guys have all
departed and the blame lies there for those who must shoulder it.
Some sort of circle of maturity is completed once this is acknowledged, and that acceptance is the price that must be paid for the
unfettered freedom of the mind. There were, indeed, dark pre-
sences in the killing field that night, but every one of them had a
human form and each of them possessed the freedom to make a
choice. The evil resides not in the act, but in the choosing.

Mea culpa, mea culpa, mea maxima culpa.

ON SATURDAY, 28 May 1977, Liam Townson was identified by
Sergeant Tiernan of the garda síochána as he sat in a parked car at
a Dundalk road check. Tiernan arrested him under Section 2 of the
controversial Emergency Powers Act 1970, a piece of schizo-
phrenic legislation which purports to defend freedom by whittling
away at its foundations. The legislation enabled gardaí to detain a
suspect for questioning for up to 7 days.

People arrested under this surreal curtailment of established
rights tend to find themselves unequal before the law, caught up in
some Kafkaesque nightmare in which violence is done to both the
dignity of man and the concept of justice.

The process soils everything it touches: those it would avenge;
the people it would condemn; the pliant tools who for reasons of
professional survival or personal aggrandisement undertake this
dirty work and, finally, the legislature which has so forgotten its
duty to what is true, pure and ennobling as to trample it into the
dust for some transient and ultimately treacherous political advantage.

143

Similar legislation exists in Britain as two nations condemn themselves to regular baths in a sewer in order to retain a cosmetic and increasingly deceptive look of cleanliness. So it is that a process of corruption, arising from a primary condition that is both stagnant and repellent, rolls on to distort men, systems and countries as it drips its slow poison into every area of national life.

That first compromise with falsity extends itself until, in the end, the falsity is the only reality that is recognisable. The graveyards of history are littered with the dishonoured bones of nations which have gone down that road.

Five months after Townson's arrest he was sentenced in the Special Criminal Court, Dublin to penal servitude for life. That happened on 10 October. The record of his trial suggests very strongly that the weight of evidence was sufficient to convict him had he been afforded the valuable right of being brought up before a jury of his peers. It is a matter for regret that Ireland's legislators were so lacking in both political maturity and confidence as to erode one of the cornerstone rights of a free and just society.

Townson was arrested just ten days after two fishermen found some spent rounds of ammunition and what appeared to be blood stains on the banks of the small river that runs through Ravensdale Park in County Louth. The whole area was in a high state of alert with considerable police and military activity on both sides of the border.

The public had also been told of the missing SAS officer, so the men reported their find that same day, 18 May 1977. Gardaí rushed to the Flurry River to find bloodstains on the side of a small bridge across the river. They were about one yard from the ground, indicating that someone had rested a bleeding head against the stones.

Detective Garda Michael Niland said he found four separate blood stains on the wall of the bridge. They were fairly close together and varied between thirty-seven and forty-one inches from the ground. The surrounding grass was trampled over a wide area and where the soil had been churned it was stained with blood.

Coins were scattered over the ground, presumably spilled from pockets in the same struggle as caused the grass to be trampled down. The find was made just one day after the Provisional IRA had claimed responsibility for Nairac's murder.

Niland also told the court that a search of the area had discovered a spent cartridge case from a 9mm Browning and a round of ammunition of the same calibre. Later on, it was claimed, Townson took detectives to Ravensdale where he showed them where Nairac's gun was stashed, and the one he had brought from Dundalk.

Further across the field he unearthed a plastic bag of clothing, discarded by the kidnap gang after they found it to be spattered with blood. The bag contained a sweater which Townson had been wearing and it was rushed away for examination.

There was also a lot of blood in the Three Steps car park. An RUC sergeant, giving evidence in a murder case for which there was no body, said there were signs of a violent struggle at the car park. The ground was covered with gravel and the blood had soaked in.

'If my memory serves me right,' he said, 'there was a pool of blood about four palms wide. The blood continued for 20 yards along the main road in the direction of Fork Hill in splashes approximately one inch square. Somebody had been bleeding vigorously'.

The court was told by the prosecution that despite the considerable quantity of blood available for forensic examination:

> We are not in a position to give evidence in relation to the blood grouping of Captain Nairac.

Forensic laboratory staff, lacking a control sample, could not match up the spilled blood and say it had been shed by Nairac, but the technicians did find a hair under one of the armpits of Townson's recovered sweater, suggesting that somebody had been held there in a headlock. British army investigators found a hairbrush belonging to Nairac in his quarters and handed it over for tests. These showed that the hair on Townson's sweater was similar to those on Nairac's brush. That was the only forensic link which gardaí could find which connected Townson to Nairac.

Townson allegedly made seven statements of admission, but when the case came to trial five of them were thrown out because the court held that his constitutional rights had been violated during questioning. His solicitor, Donal Carroll, took the unusual step of going into the witness box to testify that gardaí had obstructed him in visiting his client.

He said that he had repeatedly telephoned Dundalk garda station on both Sunday, 29 May 1977, and the following day to try to arrange a professional visit to Townson. When his calls were not returned, as promised, he drove from Dublin to Dundalk where he was kept waiting for more than three hours before being allowed to see his client.

At the end of it all Liam Townson was sentenced to penal servitude for life, mainly on the basis of two admitted statements. His defending counsel, the fluent and imaginative Patrick MacEntee, one of the senior silks at the Irish Bar, suggested that Nairac may have been heading south to assassinate somebody when apprehended by the kidnap gang.

Or he might have been going to meet informers, said Mr MacEntee.

He raised another intriguing possibility, which was that Nairac did not actually die after being shot. Instead, he lay wounded until the field cleared and then made his escape.

The judges were against him, and they announced that despite the lack of a body they believed Nairac was dead. In reaching that conclusion they were able to rely largely on Townson's own damning words.

One of the two statements the court admitted began:

I shot the British captain. He never told us anything. He was a great soldier.

The statement continued:

I had been drinking in a pub in Dundalk. Danny O'Rourke came in. He told me to get a bit of hardware that there was a job to be done ... I got my gun, a .32 revolver. I went to the bridge near the road at

Ravensdale. I fired a shot from my gun on the way out to test it ... I had a lot of drink taken.

I asked the captain who he was. I asked him who he knew. He said Seamus Murphy from Drumintee. I told him that I didn't believe him, that he was a British soldier and I had to kill him ... I hit him on the head with my fist, and then the butt of my gun.

Captain Nairac said: 'You're going to kill me. Can I have a priest?' He was in a bad state. I aimed at his head. I only put one in him. The gun misfired a few times. I left the body there and went home across the fields. I don't know where the body is, and that's the truth.

Townson got out of jail in September 1990 and went to ground. Those who know him say that he is a changed man, filled with penitence and a quiet sorrow for the savagery that led on to the death of Captain Nairac. He has, they say, rediscovered the Catholic faith of his childhood.

ROBERT NAIRAC RATTLED around the killer country of South Armagh for thirty or more months back in those turbulent days of the 1970s. He toted his adopted personality as a cardboard, cut-out Irishman through areas where he was widely recognised as some sort of renegade, a vastly amusing eccentric on permanent tour for the delight of the watchful but welcoming people of the border country.

He stood in public houses in which the spirit of republicanism lay as thick on the air as plug tobacco smoke, singing his chooky ould come-all-ye's while the saloon bar elders tittered into their pint pots and nudged each other with sly, rheumaticky elbows. Get a load of the quare fella there, they said. By the time he's done he'll have sung the whorin' border away.

After Nairac was dead there was many a one who said that they had known all along that he was a British officer in mufti, but that is a claim that lacks credibility. If that had been widely known in the supercharged, gun-law atmosphere of South Armagh the singing spy called Danny Boy would have died a lot sooner than he did.

The casebook on Robert Nairac is necessarily incomplete because he was not killed as the result of a properly planned action by the Provisional IRA. Only two of the men involved in his death, Liam Townson and Gerard Fearon, admitted IRA membership and the rest, while clearly republican sympathisers, were not acting under any sort of discipline. This was a nasty, messy, opportunist killing which bid fair to embarrass the IRA as much as it did the British army.

The Provisional IRA, a quick learner, swiftly managed to adopt the technique of suggesting it had total control of a situation it only learned of after it had been resolved. This is what it did with Nairac's killing. It took the Provos three days after Nairac's disappearance to come up with a face-saving claim that they had officially executed him.

That week's edition of their newspaper, *Republican News*, trumpeted:

> The elimination of Nairac is an obvious breakthrough in the war against the Special Air Service. Sources close to the IRA refuse to say how much detailed knowledge they now have of the SAS, but they are obviously highly pleased with what Nairac has given them or confirmed.
>
> IRA sources have revealed that Capt Nairac was a high-ranking SAS officer. When arrested he had in his possession a Browning automatic with two magazines. He pretended he had been in Canada and brought the gun home with him.
>
> When arrested he gave as his identity that of a Republican Clubs' member; this Stick identity was broken almost immediately by an IRA officer. SAS morale must now be shattered as one of their most high-ranking officers has been arrested, interrogated, executed and has disappeared without a trace.

This ranting nonsense, which manages twice to elevate Nairac, holder of a junior officer's rank, to one of the 'most high-ranking' SAS officers carefully conceals the fact that Nairac's identity did not become known to the IRA until it was revealed by the British army.

The article totally failed to address the question of why this 'high-ranking SAS officer' was allowed to roam freely around South Armagh until he was killed in a drunken attack.

Since Nairac died there have been various improbable explanations for this from the IRA. One of the most frequently heard is that the IRA allowed him free range so they could watch him and see what he was doing.

Another claim is that he was discovered to be a high profile decoy, thrown into the republican stronghold to distract attention from some other, more dangerous, operative. The naivety of such claims is matched only by that of those who expect them to be believed.

There is a very simple explanation for Nairac's immunity, and it is that the Provisionals were completely taken in by his carefully fabricated pose as a member of the Official IRA. His mock Belfast accent was generally serviceable enough to fool the casual contacts he made, and he had gathered enough background knowledge to disarm the tailored scepticism of the leery men whose business was to keep watch on passing strangers.

The Provisional and the Official IRA had just been through a bloody divorce and were slowly settling in to a period of post-connubial mutual loathing. Tactless questions could lead to more gun play as the two organisations licked their wounds and tip-toed around each other with the hostile wariness of estranged bedfellows.

Suspicion spread through the towns and villages like a creeping plague as the stealthy figures of a shifting group of spies, informers, assassins and other assorted mayhem-makers made a scabrous progress across the blighted land.

Mixed in with them were the figures of mystery republicans, men and women in flight from a turgid, eventless present. They had been drawn from all parts of Ireland, the wandering heirs of 1916 or '98, the bold Fenian men, the boys of Wexford and the girls of the County Armagh, all on the one road, seeking a rebirth of old and hallowed times. It was by adopting the nostalgic yearnings of one of these displaced romantics that the SAS man, driven by his own capricious fancies, found some sort of escapist refuge.

Captain Robert Nairac, the man from Connemara, Ardoyne,

149

McGillicuddy's Reeks but mostly God knows where, called on his building site memories to flesh out his claim to be an honest Irishman, up from the wilds of beyond and moving around this part of the country in search of a role in the patriot game. He moved among a new priesthood of death, another generation that sought national redemption through the spilled blood of its sons and daughters, not knowing that the time of his own sacrifice was drawing near.

Nairac sang 'The Broad Black Brimmer' in memory of the old times, and paraded his Sticky credentials before those who showed an interest. The fact was that he had made contact with the Official IRA in Belfast, posing as an Irishman who had developed left-wing leanings while working as a labourer in Britain.

He carried enough carelessly acquired Socialist jargon to persuade his contacts to accept him as the sort of self-taught, fustian intellectual whose sympathies lay with the coming revolution. The Official IRA had by that time abandoned the armed republican struggle in favour of a doctrinaire Marxism which was later to develop some of the nastier characteristics of the worst years of the Stalinist era.

The Official IRA's guns were never handed in to anyone since they were needed for the series of armed robberies by which the Official IRA, evolving by way of various changes of identity into the Workers Party, financed its activities. The guns were also being held against the day when the victorious workers would sweep aside the bourgeois institutions of both parts of Ireland.

It was always easy to laugh at such political credulity, though it was never advisable to do so in public for fear of a beating with hurley sticks, or worse, from the sensitive, earnest and unarmed comrades.

This abandonment of the republican cause left the Provisionals as the main focus for the fight against British occupation, although they were soon to be joined by the Irish National Liberation Army, a breakaway group of fanatical hard men from the Official IRA. All of this left the Provisionals with their security checks intact while opening up the Officials to easy infiltration. Almost all Provo recruiting was done within the Catholic ghettos where enquiries among friends and neighbours would quickly establish a person's character, attitudes and beliefs.

That had also been true of the Officials, but now their attachment to a creed of international brotherhood barred them from the sort of parish pump recruitment policies that helped protect the Provos. There was also the problem that they needed to replace the considerable number of people they had lost in their political metamorphosis. Like some sad and unfortunate woman, so abused by life as entirely to lose all sense of personal worth, they were prepared to take on all comers. Captain Nairac was one of the suitors.

He came with glib words on his lips and a carefully concealed gun in his armpit. There is some doubt as to how deeply he managed to penetrate the transformed movement, but it is certain that he was able to operate on its fringes, an unstructured lefty who hung around the drinking clubs dropping cant phrases about the dictatorship of the proletariat while his straining ears picked up names and gossip, the sluggish lifeblood of his tawdry trade.

The years have produced a series of attempts to soften the memory of Captain Robert Nairac by turning him into some sort of caring figure who went about his business of bringing peace to the troubled land of Ireland with a tender regard for the decencies, a near-saintly warrior who never once transgressed the code of an English gentleman. That, of course, is the most astonishing rubbish.

Consider the facts. Robert Nairac was commissioned into a Guards regiment, one of the world's more efficient engines of mass slaughter. From there he went on to do advanced bush training while joining the SAS for more honing as a highly skilled killer machine, one of Britain's modern Ninjas. The lurking suggestion that he then went roaming around the hills of South Armagh as some sort of harmless cultural ambassador does not sit very comfortably alongside these details.

Despite the denials of British politicians it is now clear that units of the SAS were operating in Northern Ireland by late 1970. Six years later, in January 1976, a disingenuous statement from Whitehall announced that SAS units were being sent in because of the upsurge in sectarian killing in South Armagh.

This was a cover for the reinforcements which were being sent for such secret units as 4 Field Survey Troop, whose operatives such as Nairac reported directly to London and who mostly worked on their own, without either field guidance or back-up. These men had two roles. One was to gather information and the other was to eliminate dangerous enemies by whatever means possible. Strangely, the documents for this mysterious unit were unaccountably destroyed soon after Nairac's death.

At the time Nairac took on his undercover role MI5 had ousted their somewhat more long-sighted sister service, MI6, to take over intelligence in the north. The urbane men of MI6, lethal but rather more sophisticated than their gung-ho colleagues of MI5, believed that the role of the intelligence services was to prepare for a political solution in the north. The men in MI5, known derisively as 'the blood and snot brigade' thought the IRA could be bludgeoned into submission by a series of tactical assassinations and other terrorist tactics. They sent their operatives out to kill.

Sometimes, working through the Military Reaction Force or with a loyalist murder gang, the secret SAS men did this by proxy. There were times when they had to be prepared to pull the trigger themselves. That is why Nairac carried a specially adapted 9mm Browning in an armpit holster.

This was a gun that had been drawn from the SAS ghost store of non-existent weapons. Nairac's officially issued weapon lay in his quarters at Bessbrook barracks on the night he died, and that raises some interesting questions about why, on what was apparently just another Danny Boy expedition, he needed to carry a gun that could not be traced. It may be that lawyer MacEntee's suggestion that Nairac was on his way to kill someone has some merit.

There is, though, no way of proving that Nairac was carrying the ghost gun on that night with murder in mind, since it may well have been his habit to carry it with him all the time. The conclusion of that line of argument is even more damning than the original theory.

If that is what Nairac did then the question arises as to why he preferred an untraceable gun to his perfectly serviceable issue revolver. The Browning, with its extended trigger and featherweight

152

firing action, was the perfect killer's gun. There is a clear reason for Nairac's preference. He needed to be able to kill people without being called to account for his actions. If he wished just to defend himself against attack there was no reason why he should not use his service weapon.

Nobody will ever now know how many times that 9mm Browning was used to visit death on some inconvenient or hostile person, or if it was used at all. What we may assume, though, is that Nairac was both prepared and happy to use it as the occasion arose.

In some three years of unaccountable undercover operations it would be extraordinary if he had never pulled that trigger. The political remedies prescribed for the north since 1969 have mostly consisted of some form of blood-letting. Captain Nairac was a professional shedder of blood, trained in furtive and secret practices. He was a killer on the loose. It calls for an enormous act of either credulity or faith to assume that he never employed his fatal talents.

WHEN THEY GOT word, at 05.45 hours, 15 May 1977, that an SAS officer had gone missing, the Royal Ulster Constabulary threw some two hundred men into South Armagh to aid the one hundred soldiers who were already scouring the area in search of the missing man.

Within days they had five men in custody and a dragnet out for others on whom they were never to lay a restraining hand. Just twelve months after Townson had been sentenced in Dublin the five RUC suspects appeared before a Belfast court. Their case made legal history since it was the first time anyone was tried in the north for an offence committed in the Republic.

Gerard Fearon, a 21-year-old IRA man was sentenced to life for murder. Thomas Morgan, aged 17, also found guilty of murder, was sentenced to be held indefinitely, with his release to be decided upon by the Secretary of State. Daniel O'Rourke was cleared of murder but jailed for 10 years for manslaughter. Owen Rocks got three years for withholding information and Michael McCoy five years for kidnapping.

All of them were out of prison by the time Townson was released but one of them, Morgan, was not to enjoy his liberty for long. He served nine years and was released in 1986. Just one year later he died in a crash between his Vauxhall car and a lorry on the same Newry to Dublin road down which Nairac had been driven to his death.

There were three empty spaces in the dock. Kevin Crilly, who allegedly drove the car which brought Townson to the killing field, and Pat Maguire, both left the north for the Republic. Maguire was implicated in statements admitted in the Belfast hearing.

Terry McCormick, the false priest who was alleged, in court, to have offered to hear Nairac's confession, is in the United States where he moved suddenly after the soldier's death. Despite their implication in various statements of guilt all of these men are innocent in the eyes of the law.

No attempt has been made to bring any of them to trial and so the Nairac affair, unilluminated by further disclosures, melts gently into the shadows of recent history. Dusk folds around the memory, obscuring its bitterly wrought parable about the gladiatorial use of unexamined force in an arena of moral dereliction. The message glimmers briefly in the darkness and then fades away. In doing that it writes its own epitaph on the latter years of yet another violent and inhumane century which, like all that went before, has always stood ready to smile forgivingly on its own ferocities.

BIBLIOGRAPHY

The SAS in Ireland, Raymond Murray, Mercier Press, Dublin and Cork 1990.

Contact, A.F.N. Clarke, Secker and Warburg, London 1983.

The SAS (Official History), Philip Warner, Sphere Books, London 1983.

Rogue Warrior of the SAS, Roy Bradford and Martin Dillon, Arrow Books, London 1989.

Inside the British Army, Anthony Beevor, Corgi Books, London 1991.

Ambush, the war between the SAS and the IRA, James Adams, Robin Morgan and Anthony Bambridge, Pan Books, London 1988.

Gangs and counter-gangs, Frank Kitson, Barrie and Rockliffe, London 1960.

Bunch of Fives, Frank Kitson, Faber and Faber, London 1977.

Directing Operations, Frank Kitson, Faber and Faber, London 1989.

Warfare as a Whole, Frank Kitson, Faber and Faber, London 1987.

Chink, Lavinia Greacy, Papermac, London 1989.

Invisible Armies: Terrorism into the 1990s, Stephen Segaller, Sphere Books, London 1987.

A History of the British Secret Service, Richard Deacon, Muller, London 1970.

The Other Face of Terror, Ray Hill with Andrew Bell, Grafton Books, London 1988.

Terrorism, Walter Laquer, Abacus, London 1978.

Beating the Terrorists, Peter Taylor, Penguin, London, 1980.

The Dictionary of Espionage, Christopher Dobson and Ronald Payne, Grafton Books, London 1986.

The Second Oldest Profession: The Spy as Bureaucrat, Patriot, Fantasist and Whore, Phillip Knightly, Pan Books, London 1986.

The Climate of Treason, Andrew Boyle, Coronet Books, London 1980.

MI5, John Bulloch, Corgi Books, London 1963.

The Real World of Spies, Charles Wighton, Fontana Books,

London 1965.

Who Framed Colin Wallace?, Paul Foot, Pan Books, London 1989.

War Without Honour, Fred Holroyd and Nick Burridge, The Medium Publishing Company, Hull 1989.

Inquests and Disputed Killings in Northern Ireland, pamphlet produced in 1992 by the Committee on the Administration of Justice, Belfast.

Affaire Irland contre Royaume Uni. Text of the judgment of the European Court of Human Rights which condemned interrogation techniques in Northern Ireland as 'inhuman and degrading', Strasbourg 1977.

The Dirty War, Martin Dillon, Arrow Books, London 1991.

The Shankill Butchers, Martin Dillon, Arrow Books, London 1990.

Ten Dead Men, David Beresford, Grafton Books, London 1987.

Broadening the Battlefield: The H Blocks and the Rise of Sinn Féin, Liam Clarke, Gill and Macmillan, Dublin 1987.

The IRA, Tim Pat Coogan, Fontana, London 1974.

The Provisional IRA, Patrick Bishop and Eamonn Mallie, Corgi Books, London 1989.

The Secret Army, J. Bowyer Bell, Academy Press, Dublin 1970.

Bloody Sunday in Derry, Eamonn McCann with Maureen Shiels and Bridie Hannigan, Brandon, Dingle, Co. Kerry 1992.

Rebels: The Irish Rising of 1916, Peter de Rossa, Corgi Books, London 1991.

The British Campaign in Ireland, 1919–21, Charles Townshend, Oxford University Press 1980.

A Terrible Beauty is Born, Ulick O'Connor, Panther Books, London 1985.

Ireland's Civil War, Carlton Younger, Muller, London 1968.

The Civil War, 1922–23, Eoin Neeson, Poolbeg Press, Dublin 1989.

Harry, Uinseann Mac Eoin, Argenta Publications, Dublin 1985.

On Another Man's Wound, Ernie O'Malley, Rich and Cowan, London 1936.

War in an Irish Town, Eamonn McCann, Pluto Press, London 1980.

Blind Justice, Joe Joyce and Peter Murtagh, Poolbeg Press, Dublin 1984.

Round Up the Usual Suspects, Derek Dunne and Gene Kerrigan, Magill Publications Ltd., Dublin 1984.

Arming the Protestants, Michael Farrell, Pluto Press, London 1983.

Northern Ireland: The Orange State, Michael Farrell, Pluto Press, London 1985

The Politics of Irish Freedom, Gerry Adams, Brandon, Dingle, Co. Kerry 1987.

Connolly's Marxism, Bernard Ransom, Pluto Press, London 1980.

Northern Ireland and the Algerian Analogy, Hugh Roberts, Athol Books, Belfast 1986.

British Brutality in Ireland, Jack O'Brien, Mercier Press, Dublin and Cork 1989.

Ireland Since the Famine, F.S.L. Lyons, Weidenfeld and Nicolson, London 1986.

Facts and Figures of the Belfast Pogrom, 1920–22, G.B. McKenna, O'Connell Publishing Co., Dublin 1925.

The Great Dan, Charles Chenevix Trench, Grafton Books, London 1984.

Tudor and Stuart Ireland, Margaret MacCurtain, Gill and Macmillan, Dublin1972.

A History of Ireland in the 18th Century, W.E.H. Lecky, Longman, Green and Co., London 1913.

The Colonizer and the Colonized, Albert Memmi, Souvenir Press, London 1974.

British Imperialism in the Nineteenth Century, ed. C.C. Eldridge, Macmillan, London 1984.

The Great Game, Peter Hopkirk, Oxford University Press 1990.

Amritsar: The Massacre that ended the Raj, Alfred Draper, Cassell, London 1981.

The Indivisible Island, Frank Gallagher, Gollancz, London 1957.

The 'B' Specials, Sir Arthur Hezlet, Tom Stacey, London 1972.

The Green Flag (three volumes), Robert Kee, Penguin, London 1972.

    Volume 1: *The Most Distressful Country*

Volume 2: *The Bold Fenian Men*
Volume 3: *Ourselves Alone*
The Strange Death of Liberal England, George Dangerfield, Paladin, London 1982.
Smear: Wilson and the Secret State, Stephen Dorill and Robin Ramsay, Fourth Estate Ltd., London 1991.
The Wilson Plot: The Intelligence Service and the Discrediting of a Prime Minister, David Leigh, William Heinemann, London 1988.
Northern Ireland: A Personal Perspective, Merlyn Rees, Methuen, London 1985.
The State in Northern Ireland, Paul Bew, *et al,* University Press, Manchester 1979.
The Mountain Can Move, Christopher M. Hussey, Dunesk Press, Dublin 1985.
The Widening Gulf, Dennis Kennedy, Blackstaff Press, Belfast 1987.
The Nairac Affair, Mícheál Ó Cuinneagáin 1979.

More Interesting Titles

THE SAS IN IRELAND
Raymond Murray

Traces the history of the British Army Special Services Regiment, the SAS in Ireland over the last twenty years. It details their activities – intelligence gathering and surveillance, their links with British Intelligence, notably MI5 and MI6, their connection with sectarian murders and many other deaths.

ONE DAY IN MY LIFE
Bobby Sands

One Day in My Life is a human document of suffering, determination, anguish, courage and faith. It also portrays frightening examples of man's inhumanity to man.

'I wish it were possible to ensure that those in charge of formulating British policy in Ireland would read these pages. They might begin to understand the deep injuries which British policy has inflicted upon this nation, and now seek to heal these wounds.'

From the Introduction by Seán MacBride.

BOBBY SANDS and the Tragedy of Northern Ireland
John M. Feehan

The life of Bobby Sands, from his childhood to his death in jail after 66 days on hunger strike. The author deals at length with all the efforts made by the church, state and others to induce Bobby Sands to come off the hunger strike.

MICHAEL COLLINS AND THE TREATY
His differences with de Valera
T. Ryle Dwyer

To Michael Collins the signing of the Treaty between Ireland and Britain in 1921 was a 'stepping stone'. Eamon de Valera called it 'Treason'.

The controversy surrounding this Treaty is probably the most important single factor in the history of this country, and T. Ryle Dwyer not only takes an in-depth look at the characters and motivations of the two main Irish protagonists but also gives many insights into the views and ideas of the other people involved on both sides of the Irish Sea.

THE COURSE OF IRISH HISTORY
Edited by T.W. Moody and F.X. Martin

This highly acclaimed book is the first of its kind in its field. It provides a rapid short survey, with a geographical introduction, of the whole course of Ireland's history. Based on a series of Radio Telefís Éireann television programmes it is designed to be both popular and authoritative, concise but comprehensive, highly selective but balanced and fair-minded, critical but constructive and sympathetic. A distinctive feature is its wealth of illustrations.

Milestones in Irish History
Edited by Liam de Paor

This book spans the whole range of time from early prehistory to the present and discusses the great turning points in the history of Ireland, their causes and their consequences.